THE

MONOPOLY BRAND

COMPANION

THE
MONOPOLY
BRAND
COMPANION

THE PLAYERS' GUIDE

The Game from A to Z • Winning Tips • Trivia

By **MR. MONOPOLY**
as told to **PHILIP ORBANES**

STERLING

New York / London
www.sterlingpublishing.com

STERLING and the distinctive Sterling logo
are registered trademarks of Sterling Publishing Co., Inc.

Library of Congress Cataloging-in-Publication Data Available

10   9   8   7   6   5   4   3   2   1

Published by Sterling Publishing Co., Inc.
387 Park Avenue South, New York, NY 10016
© 2007 by Philip Orbanes
Distributed in Canada by Sterling Publishing
c/o Canadian Manda Group, 165 Dufferin Street
Toronto, Ontario, Canada M6K 3H6
Distributed in the United Kingdom by GMC Distribution Services
Castle Place, 166 High Street, Lewes, East Sussex, England BN7 1XU
Distributed in Australia by Capricorn Link (Australia) Pty. Ltd.
P.O. Box 704, Windsor, NSW 2756, Australia

Printed in China
All rights reserved

Sterling ISBN-13: 978-1-4027-5406-7
          ISBN-10: 1-4027-5406-X

For information about custom editions, special sales, premium and
corporate purchases, please contact Sterling Special Sales Department
at 800-805-5489 or specialsales@sterlingpublishing.com.

CONTENTS

Foreword   vii

Acknowledgments   ix

One: How It All Began   1

In which we visit Mr. Monopoly, learn the story behind the birth of the
Monopoly game, and meet Charles Darrow, the "father" of the game.

Two: The Rules Explained   27

In which the game's objective, equipment, and methods of standard
Monopoly play are outlined in detail, and we learn, among other
things, exactly why, officially, you don't collect money when you land
on Free Parking.

Three: A Trip Around the Board   53

In which Mr. Monopoly visits Boardwalk, Park Place, and the famous
spaces—as well as their real life counterparts in Atlantic City—and
in which the master tries his hand at his namesake game.

Four: The Winning Touch   111

In which Mr. Monopoly shares his very own foolproof, thirteen-step
system of winning at the Monopoly game.

Five: A Monopoly Party and Some
New Ways to Play   129

In which Mr. and Mrs. Monopoly's home comes to life and hosts
the social event of the season—and Mr. Monopoly reveals some
exciting variations on standard play.

Six: Tournament Monopoly   141

In which we enter the exciting world of high-risk, high-stakes
Monopoly play, and relive many breathtaking moments in
tournament competition history.

Seven: In the Words of the Champions   171

In which the world's best Monopoly players offer their secret
playing tips.

Eight: Exciting New Versions of Play,
Monopoly Records   179

In which we sample Monopoly games from around the world,
officially licensed versions, and highlight the latest versions of the
game, some of which take it to even greater heights.

Nine: The Monopoly Quiz   187

In which Mr. Monopoly tests your mastery of the game.

Ten: Return to "The World's Playground"   199

In which we take a special excursion on the Boardwalk Flyer
and travel back in time.

Index   205

FOREWORD

My grandfather, George S. Parker, first introduced me to Mr. Monopoly when I was just a toddler in the 1930s. I liked him from the start. My father, Robert B. M. Barton, was president of Parker Brothers at the time and the word "monopoly" was heard as frequently in our household back then as it was when I became president of the firm in 1973.

Though I retired in 1984, Mr. Monopoly is still going strong, vowing never to retire! Since his first association with the Monopoly game in 1936, Mr. Monopoly has become known and appreciated by millions. Today, he and the game are synonymous. Take it from me; Mr. Monopoly knows this great game inside and out. Yet, before this book, his knowledge had gone untapped.

We now have Phil Orbanes to thank for finally persuading this legendary character to take the time to share his wit and wisdom with us all. A friend of mine for many years, Phil is a longtime admirer of both the Monopoly game and Mr. Monopoly.

So sit back, relax, and read everything you ever wanted to know about the world's most famous board game.

When you're done, keep it with your copy of the Monopoly game. You'll want to refer to it whenever you play. That's why Mr. Monopoly has named it *The Monopoly Companion.*

Randolph P. Barton
Former President
Parker Brothers

ACKNOWLEDGMENTS

Mr. Monopoly wishes to thank the following friends and associates for all their help, over the years, in the preparation of the three editions of this book: Randolph and Robert B. M. Barton, Oliver Howes, Laura Pecci, Anna Orbanes (for the recipes!), Janine Giglio, Pat McGovern, Evelyn Cuoco, George Fox, Louis Vanne, Neil Sumner, Bill Conlon, Tony Lemone, Rene Soriano, Sid Sackson, Dave Sadowski, Sheryl F. Schulz, Donna Whitney, Chris Williamson, Holy Richl, Penny Grieci, Cameron Nixon, George Burtch, Tom Dusenberry, and the Literary Group.

He would also like to express a note of thanks to Madge for her patience through the year, and to nephews Andy, Randy, and Sandy for their enthusiasm over the gameboards.

Philip Orbanes would like to thank Bunny and Bea for that memorable first game, and to the following players: Anna, Philip, Julian, Donna, Kathy, and Matthew.

AN UNEXPECTED INVITATION

The phone rang early one Saturday morning. My wife, up earlier than me as usual, picked up in the bedroom and said hello. I opened one eye just wide enough to see the look of amazement consuming her face. "What is it?" I said, half hoping it was nothing much and that I could let my eyelid fall shut once more.

"It's him!" she replied in a hush. "Here, take the phone."

"Who?" I protested, now up on one elbow.

"Mr. Monopoly®!"

In disbelief, I bolted out of bed and juggled the phone as she handed it off to me. I raised it to my ear and tried to sound fully awake. "Hello . . . Good morning . . ."

A vibrant, authoritative voice flowed into my eardrum. "And good morning to you. Listen, young man, you've been as determined as anyone, and what you had to say in your last letter found favor with me. So I'll do it."

"Do it? You mean grant me the interview?"

"Did you ask for anything else?"

"No," I replied, feeling slightly foolish, the last wave of drowsiness receding from my body. "The interview is all I need. It would be a great honor."

"Yes I know. You said that in all your letters. But it's not that. I just feel the time is right to tell the rich story of the Monopoly game. And to give everyone a chance to learn what I know about the game, which is really everything. So I'll grant the interview and a lot more."

"This is terrific. You'll make a lot of people very happy. How soon can we start?"

"How soon can you get to Atlantic City?"

Because the bustling city was no longer dependent on the famous railroads that held fast on each side of the Monopoly board, I had to touch down in an airliner in nearby Pomona. I lamented not arriving in a sleek coach after it sped over the salt marshes separating Atlantic City from the Jersey mainland.

I found a cab waiting and jumped inside. I unfolded the piece of paper in my jacket pocket and called out our destination. The driver turned and smiled—he was an old-timer with an unruly fringe of white hair surrounding a battered fishing cap—"Mr. Monopoly's place, eh? He's a famous one, he is. Got his picture on all those game boxes. I've seen him in those TV commercials too. Yes indeed, that man's in tall cotton."

"Do you know much about him?" I asked as we pulled onto the Atlantic City Expressway. Ahead loomed the famous skyline, pierced by the glittering casino-hotels.

"Nah, but I know all about the game."

We drove over a bridge and entered the city.

"I'll tell you my secrets."

"Please do."

"Ya gotta buy Free Parking 'cause all the money goes there. And always get immunity when you make a trade. Oh, yeah, don't forget you can't build hotels until the houses are gone."

I was about to offer some contrary opinions when I noticed the driver had made a sharp turn onto Ventnor Avenue and the tall buildings began to recede behind me. I gave the address again. "It's in Marvin Gardens," I offered helpfully.

"I know where it is. And it ain't Mar-vin Gardens. It's M-a-r-v-e-n. It's outside the city proper. There ain't no such thing as Mar-vin Gardens."

His last comment, I was to learn, was the only knowledge he had gotten straight concerning the game.

"That fella got it spelled wrong. Name was Darrow. He took a chance and made the game years ago. Clarence Darrow. There's a plaque for him on the Boardwalk."

"I believe his name was Charles Darrow. That other Darrow was an attorney famous for his legal defense of evolution."

"Well, this Darrow fella made things evolve too. That Mr. Monopoly fella can tell you all about that."

"That's why I'm here."

We turned onto a beautiful curvilinear street in a compound called Marven Gardens, with an "e." Tall trees sheltered stately mansions of brick and stucco. We slowed and pulled into the drive of one of them. "Went past here a dozen times," the driver said as I paid the bill. "Never dropped anyone off here afore."

My tap on the shiny brass ring gracing the front door was greeted by the same vibrant voice I'd first heard on the phone. "Be right there young man."

The door opened. There he stood: Mr. Monopoly. I looked down and accepted his hand, charmed by the twinkle in his blue eyes and the grin peeking out beneath the outrageous mustache and rosy cheeks. "Come in, come in. This way. Get off your feet and have a seat. I have many homes, but this is the most appropriate one in which to hold a conversation about the Monopoly game."

A dog's bark interrupted him and into the foyer dashed a little black-haired terrier. Mr. Monopoly scooped him up in one hand and held him across his forearm. "Scotty, say hello to our guest."

Mr. Monopoly led me into a walnut-paneled library with shelves sporting hundreds of books. I looked up to see a handsome balcony along the rear wall, accessible by a spiral stairway. As I walked into the library, I noticed photos of him everywhere. In one, he was shaking Charles Darrow's hand; in another, kissing the hand of Miss America. Dozens of Monopoly games filled a glass-door cabinet. "I have a copy of every edition," he noted proudly as we sat down. "I especially like the newer sets because my picture's on the cover." Scotty used the moment to escape from his grasp and race out of the library. Mr. Monopoly chuckled and then called for his wife.

A pleasant woman in a long dress entered with a tray of drinks. I was introduced to his wife, Madge. I couldn't help but notice that the sturdy woman was several inches taller than her husband.

We exchanged a few words and then she said to her husband, "Now you be good and don't talk this nice gentleman's ear off."

"I'm afraid I've got him cornered, Madge," said Mr. Monopoly.

"I'm a willing prisoner. Thanks for consenting to tell what you know," I said.

"Don't let him sidetrack you," Madge warned. "He'll tell you he's the only thing that matters about the Monopoly game." Mr. Monopoly laughed and winked at her; she turned and walked out of the library.

"Well, I imagine the best place to start is at the beginning," Mr. Monopoly said, settling back in his ample leather armchair. Tell me, do you know how the Monopoly game got its start?"

I felt remarkably lucky. We were beginning our interview on a subject I could discuss.

"Charles Darrow had something important to do with it," I said confidently.

My companion smiled. "He certainly did. But there's more. So pay attention."

Mr. Monopoly looked towards the photo of he and Darrow shaking hands. "Charlie was a heck of a nice guy and he deserved to make money from the game." He rose and walked over to the gold frame and carefully lifted it from its perch; he brought it to where I was sitting. I glanced into the bright eyes and toothy grin of the sturdy man whose balding head reflected tiny lights—probably from the camera's bulb—as he shook hands with the shortish, nattily dressed financier whom I'd come to see. In the photo's background I noticed a wreath with an indecipherable message.

Mr. Monopoly satisfied my curiosity. "It says, 'Welcome to the team.' This photo was taken in 1936, the day I joined the Monopoly game. It was also the first time I met Charlie."

"What was he like?"

"Physically he was a bear of a man, but always pleasant and gentle." He aligned the photo with the others, then began to walk around the room. "Many don't know that the predecessor of the Monopoly game took root long before Charlie took the risk of making it. There were stories in the newspapers. I've got a curious nature, so I made it my business to piece together the facts." He leaned against his reading table and looked me square in the eyes. "So the answer to your earlier question is 'yes.' I can straighten out the facts."

"Good. I'm all ears."

"OK. Keep them open. I've got a lot to say."

I listened. Here's what he said.

THE STORY

The popular story about the creation of the Monopoly game goes like this:

The time is 1933. Franklin Roosevelt is president; he and the nation struggle to deal with the hardships imposed by the terrible Depression. Among the countless people affected is an unemployed heating sales representative named Charles Darrow who lives in the Germantown section of western Philadelphia in an area known as Mt. Airy. Like most people from Philadelphia, he loves to vacation at Atlantic City—the nation's most famous beach resort—about seventy miles away on the Jersey Shore. Back then, there was superb high-speed train service from Philly to Atlantic City. It was easy to jump on a Pennsy or Reading passenger train and find your toes in the warm, white sand of the beach in about an hour's time.

But in 1933, Darrow could no longer afford the $1.50 ticket to the "World's Playground," as Atlantic City was called. The lack of money and enjoyment led him to dream of both. And his dreams inspired him to invent a game.

He places a piece of circular oilcloth on his kitchen table and sketches out a gameboard. He sets up an old typewriter and types up rules, title deed cards, play money. He goes to a nearby lumber-yard and returns with some scraps of wooden moldings and free paint samples. He uses them to make little houses and hotels. Finally, he adds a pair of dice and some colored buttons for tokens.

Out comes the Monopoly game.

His family loves it. So do his friends. They all want copies. Charlie consents to make them by hand. It takes him all day to make one game and he charges $4.00 for each. More and more people play his game and they love it; Charlie can't keep up with the demand, so he pays a printer friend to print the black lines and copy on his oilcloth gameboards and on the game's cards, then colors them by hand. Production is now up to a whopping six copies a day.

Darrow figures he's onto something big, so he copyrights the game and submits it by mail to Parker Brothers in 1934. The executives in Salem, Massachusetts, like the game but feel it's too complicated for the mass market, so they reject it. Parker Brothers tells Charlie the game has a lot of playing errors—to dramatize the point, they tell him there are "fifty-two" in all!

Disappointed but not deterred, Darrow decides to risk all he has and go into production himself. He orders fully printed copies of the Monopoly game from his printer—Patterson and White—who agree to extend him the needed credit, and he begins to sell the games to local stores and the FAO Schwarz toy shop in New York. The games sell well. News of the success reaches Parker Brothers and the company puts principle aside and licenses the game from Darrow. In 1935 the Monopoly game becomes America's best-selling game. By 1936, Parker Brothers can barely keep up with the demand. All game sales records are broken.

Darrow retires a millionaire; Parker Brothers goes on to sell over 250,000,000 copies around the world of the game that started with a dream and a piece of oilcloth.

"Nice story, isn't it?" Mr. Monopoly offered.

"As American as apple pie," I replied.

"And much of it is true. Darrow was, indeed, the key player in the launch of the Monopoly game. He risked his meager savings to bring it to market. And his crucial achievement was to create the look and feel of the game. Charlie's design connected with game players. Similar games, made in prior years, lacked this essential ingredient of success."

"How did he come across the basic idea? What about the predecessor you mentioned? How long did it take for Parker Brothers to acquire all the rights to Monopoly?"

"Ah, three key questions. Let's refill our drinks and I'll answer them all."

THE ORIGIN OF THE MONOPOLY GAME

Here is what Mr. Monopoly had to say.

Great games as intricate as the Monopoly game just don't spring forth from the mind of a daydreamer. Ask any game inventor and they'll tell you just how difficult it is to come up with a really new game, as involved and carefully balanced as the Monopoly game. There's the escalating rents, the limited number of houses and hotels, the mortgage figures, and all the other finely honed values. It takes time to get these numbers right, not to mention the basic structure of a gameboard with exactly forty spaces, precisely twenty-eight of which are properties that can be purchased by the players. The game may seem second nature to us all now, but isn't it curious that no other game of its intricacy has ever appeared to rival the Monopoly game? That's because, like I said, it takes time to perfect a great game like this one.

In fact, it took years,

About thirty years in all.

That's right, the story of the Monopoly game began near the turn of the century.

So who sparked the idea behind the Monopoly game, you ask? The right question is not who, but rather *how many* people had a hand in shaping its predecessors?

TAX AND THE LADY

Real estate games date from the late 1800s, but the first known person in our trail of inventors was a woman named Elizabeth Magie (pronounced "Ma-gee"). Elizabeth was a very liberated woman for her day, and very much a free spirit. She had a real passion for whatever she did, including male impersonation. (After her  marriage, it pleased her to come to their front door dressed as a boy and fool her own husband!) In 1904, for reasons I'll soon explain, she patented a game titled the Landlord's Game. Take a look at its gameboard, as pictured on her patent.

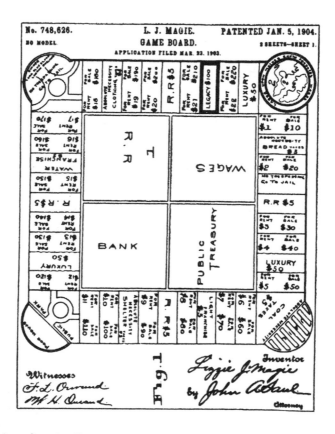

Notice the similarities to the Monopoly game: a continuous path of forty spaces; four railroads, one centered on each side; two utilities—a water and electric franchise; twenty-two other rental properties, the value of which increases constantly as one travels clockwise around the board. There are other similarities: a park space, a jail, a GO TO JAIL space. Luxury Tax is present, but not the spaces we know as Chance and Community Chest. The board's initial space, where a wage was paid, was called "Mother Earth" instead of Go.

Intriguing, isn't it? But even more so when you realize that Lizzie Magie wasn't attempting to create a best-selling board game. Instead, she came up with the Landlord's Game for propaganda reasons. At the time, she was a big supporter of the so-called "Single Tax" advocated by economist Henry George. His idea was that the only thing that should be taxed was land—real estate—thus, the "Single Tax." Magie's game didn't get much public endorsement, but she did produce it herself and sold it in shops in Maryland. Later, she moved to Illinois and took her game with her, selling it in the Chicago area.

In 1924, Elizabeth Magie-Phillips (she married Albert Phillips many years prior) revised her game and decided to approach Parker Brothers, a firm that had already published a modest-selling game of hers called Mock Trial. There she renewed her acquaintance with the man she referred to as "the King of Games"—George Parker, founder of the forty-year-old firm.

As a sixteen-year-old, he had begun selling his first creation, a game he'd devised in high school called Banking. Sales of the game were encouraging and George asked his two older brothers to join him to form a company. George believed there was an enormous market for games that were actually fun to play. Previously, board games were primarily intended for moral reinforcement, in contrast to playing cards, which were thought to be the devil's work (due to their common evolution with the tarot). But "fun" was waiting to be discovered and Parker hit a responsive chord. By 1924 his firm had sold millions of games. When Magie-Phillips came to visit, he studied her game carefully and quickly realized it wasn't fun at all—just political and educational. From experience, he knew that combination spelled failure in the marketplace. He politely declined her game, but suggested she secure patent protection once more. (What foresight! as you'll see.)

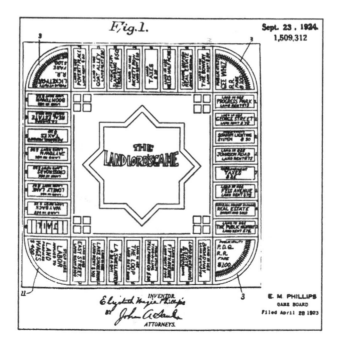

Take a look at her new gameboard. She's made a lot of changes. Three railroads have taken over corner spaces; Jail is displaced; GO TO JAIL has disappeared; the utilities now number three in all. The remaining rental properties now have names, like Easy Street, Fifth Avenue, and Lonely Lane.

Of greater importance is a rule she added to the play of the game. Her new "monopoly" rule and "Monopoly" card granted higher rents to a player who owned either all three utilities or all three railroads. She also added chips to the game. These were used to improve properties, increasing their rents.

Sound familiar?

Strictly speaking, the Monopoly game got its start the day Elizabeth Magie began to sell her Landlord's Game in 1904. While her game wasn't a commercial success, it did find its way into the economic departments of colleges in areas of the country near where she had resided: Maryland, eastern Pennsylvania, and Illinois.

Within these collegiate environments, the game was avidly played. It is known that the Landlord's Game was a favorite at schools such as the University of Pennsylvania, Princeton, Haverford, and the

University of Chicago. During this time came the improvements that transformed the Landlord's Game into the Monopoly game. This great event preceded the 1924 revision of the Landlord's Game when Elizabeth improved her game to reflect some of the changes she knew were being made to her original. You can imagine the game's early players putting aside her notion of the Single Tax. Rather than education, they wanted excitement. They sought what George Parker envisioned: fun. The questions asked were, "What if the properties were organized into groups, like the railroads?" "What if you could trade deeds? "What if the rents rose when you owned all the properties of a group?" And finally, "What if you could improve properties like in real life? You know, put buildings on them!"

Voilà!

So much for the noble pursuit of the Single Tax. Bring on the thrill of investing, the chance to make a killing. The chance to wipe out your friends!

Local street names were adopted from whatever towns the game was played, inspired by Magie-Phillips's use of curiously named streets in her original game. By the mid-1920s, this bold new game became informally known by several names, including the Monopoly game, after the most important feature of its play.

While many people in a few states remember playing handmade copies of the game during this time, the names of those who helped spread its awareness are largely lost to history, aside from economic professors like Scott Nearing, Rex Tugwell, and Roy Striker. Thus, all I can do is honor the game's many early torchbearers in general, and say, "Thank you. You did millions of people a good turn by keeping the game's flame burning."

"Wow, that's fascinating! Did Darrow learn the Landlord's Game at a local college?" I asked.

The knowing twinkle returned to his eyes. "No. He didn't know that crowd. His business was steam radiators."

"So how did he learn the game? It must have been through someone who knew someone at a college, according to what you said."

Mr. Monopoly laughed jovially. "Absolutely. Let me tell you how the Monopoly game came to be published."

CHARLES DARROW AND THE MONOPOLY GAME

Darrow came across the game in 1933. But the game he played didn't originate at nearby Princeton or Haverford. The version he embraced bore the names of streets and places from Atlantic City.

Yet its journey had started in Indiana! A teacher from Indiana-
polis named Ruth Hoskins had moved to Atlantic City. One
Christmas, she brought a copy back with her, based on a similar
game on the market in Indiana, made by a firm called Knapp
Electric. Knapp had purchased a version called Finance from a
former college student named Dan Layman. Take a look at
its board.

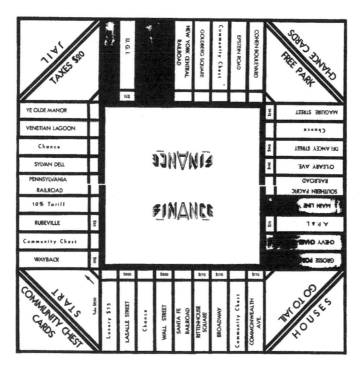

Layman was advised to call his game Finance to make it
distinct. He carried forward Lizzie's rather abstract design for its

board; there were no pictures on it. But if you look at his board, you'll clearly see the footprint of the Monopoly game. In the rules, sets of like-colored properties were called "series." "Start" was the name of the initial space. Chance and Community Chest were part of the game; their rewards and penalties were similar to those in the Monopoly game. Houses and hotels were important features of play. In fact, the game played very much like the Monopoly game. The biggest difference was that you had to auction a property when first landed on; the landing player could not buy it automatically, as there were no fixed prices for the properties. While a student of Williams College in Pennsylvania, he learned to play the Landlord's Game thanks to a friend named Louis Thun, who ran a gaming club. Layman thought it might find a market. How did a maker of electrical toys named Knapp Electric get Finance? Well, Dan Layman had a connection that knew of the firm.

Layman led to one of the last links in our chain: Ruth Hoskins. She had just gotten her job in Atlantic City, New Jersey. Together with her friends, she made a new gameboard using Atlantic City street names. They were a close-knit group of Quakers and they played this game regularly. Copies were made. One of these found its way into the hands of an old high school classmate of Darrow's wife, Esther. His name was Todd, Charles Todd. He ran into Esther and her husband Charles while they were strolling one evening in the Germantown section of Philadelphia. He soon invited them to his house for dinner and a "go" at the game. My friend Charlie was instantly taken by it.

Darrow had met his destiny.

It wasn't long before Darrow created his own version of the game. He sketched out a gameboard on the circular oilcloth used to cover his dining room table. He had a typewriter and he used it to type up deeds and cards. He made houses and hotels from scraps of wood moldings and purchased some play money. Fortuitously, unlike others who had changed the street names to match those in their area, Darrow retained the Atlantic City street names. Perhaps this is because he, like millions of his day, regarded the city as a sort of paradise. Todd had misspelled the yellow property named Marven Gardens. Darrow didn't know of the real Marven Gardens (few did), so he innocently continued the Marvin Gardens misspelling on his gameboard. One of the reasons I liked Charlie was because his instincts were good. Keeping the names of the streets the same was a real stroke of genius. After all, when you think about it, there must have been dozens of different sets of street names. But Atlantic City was created in the 1850s with the idea of making it "America's City." That's why the names of existing states were used for its streets. So Darrow instinctively retained the national image of the game, much to his credit.

Of even greater significance, Darrow created the famous icons that adore the game to this day: the corner symbols, the pictures on the board, the rectangular color bands at the top of each property's space. Collectively, these made the game friendly and appealing to everyday Americans, not just the college crowd.

Darrow's first printed copies sold well in the fall of 1934. When news reached Parker Brothers of his achievement, they recanted and made the most important deal in their history.

"So who alerted Parker Brothers? I mean, there were other game companies. How did Parker get the edge?"

"Fate," replied Mr. Monopoly, "and from remarkably close quarters."

Helen Coolidge, a friend of Sally Barton (George's daughter and wife of the firm's president, Robert Barton), telephoned to say she had purchased the game in Philadelphia that was "all the rage," adding, "It's quite something!" Sally then told her husband.

Robert Barton paid attention to his wife. He called Darrow and arranged a meeting in the firm's sales office at the Flatiron Building at 23rd and Broadway in New York. Barton had vacationed in Atlantic City several times. He and Darrow got along well. They were destined to become good friends.

An agreement was reached the next day.

The Monopoly game could not have arrived at a more critical time for Parker Brothers. By the end of 1934, times were tough for the fifty-year-old firm. The Depression had sapped the nation's discretionary income, and the game industry was hit hard. Before the Monopoly game, Barton was trying to drum up *printing* business from Boston area businesses. Within one year of his deal with Darrow, Barton had to shut down production on all other games because his printing presses couldn't keep up with the Monopoly game's demand, even working around the clock!

THE MAN WHO BOUGHT MONOPOLY

Parker Brothers purchased Darrow's copyright and helped him to patent the Monopoly game in 1935. In return, he received a royalty for every game sold. But the game's immense success caused the forerunners of the Monopoly game to come forward.

The man at the helm of Parker Brothers handled the situation brilliantly and honorably.

Robert Barton attended Harvard and while there met his wife-to-be, Sally Parker. Both of Sally's brothers had died in the 1920s. In 1932, concerned about the family's continuity in the firm he had started, George Parker asked Robert Barton—then a young Baltimore attorney—to join the firm.

He became the right man, in the right place, when the Monopoly game appeared on the scene.

When Darrow applied for his patent, the attorneys conducted a search and discovered Elizabeth Magie-Phillips's patents. George Parker recalled the memorable lady. Robert Barton dispatched his father-in-law to her home in Virginia to arrange for the purchase of her current patent.

At about the same time, Parker Brothers learned of Knapp's Finance game. And because he liked the name Fortune, Barton had Parker Brothers issue a version by that name.

Barton knew the importance of establishing a clear, solid title to his powerful seller. Without delay, he came to terms with the owner of Finance and combined it with Fortune. The patent George Parker acquired from Magie-Phillips was invaluable, because the true forerunner of all games brought to Parker's attention was the Landlord's Game. Part of the eventual agreement with Magie-Phillips stipulated that Parker Brothers would publish several of her games, which the firm did a few years later (alas, they didn't sell well, even with her name and picture on the box covers). Eventually Fortune was dropped and the Finance game reemerged. It was published until the 1970s.

In early 1936, Charles Darrow and Elizabeth Magie-Phillips were given joint credit by Parker Brothers for the establishment of the Monopoly game.

By late 1936, things calmed down. The Monopoly game was here to stay. In fact, Parker Brothers' great rival, the Milton Bradley Company, even licensed the Monopoly game's patents for their soon-to-be-famous Easy Money. In time, the Monopoly game spread around the world. Today, it is the most famous game in the world.

"So that's the way it was."

"Indeed"

"Except for one thing."

"What's that?" the little man asked in mild surprise.

"You haven't said a thing about yourself yet."

"Oh, I was like icing on the cake. You see, the Monopoly game was off to such a great start when Parker Brothers purchased it, they didn't change any visual aspect of it. They did rewrite Darrow's rules for added clarity, and included a short version of play because they still felt the game was too long." He got up and opened a cabinet,

producing a copy of the original 1935 board. "Here's what it used to look like. Much the same as today's version, see?"

"But by 1936, it was time to spruce it up a bit, so I was asked to join the team. The treasure chest was added to the board, and my picture appeared on the Chance and Community Chest cards. A few years ago, they realized I had quite a following, so they began to put my picture on every box and gameboard they make." He pointed to recent editions on his shelves.

"Handsome, don't you think?"

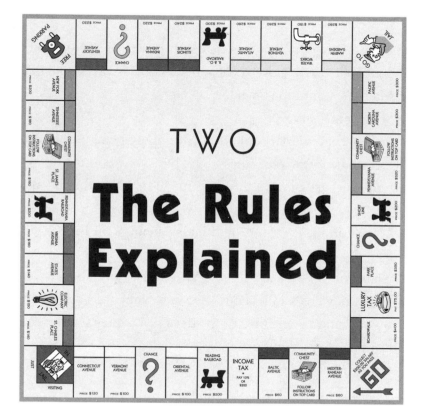

TWO

The Rules Explained

WINNING

"If you don't know how to drive a car, how can you win a race?" Mr. Monopoly asked as we reconvened. We were at work again after Madge's sumptuous meal.

"Your point being?"

"Simply that many people play Monopoly game not really knowing what the correct rules are. That's why so many games never end, because players throw in made-up rules that invariably make the game longer."

"You mean like putting the Bank's earnings on Free Parking?"

"That's one. There are others. We'll talk more about them later. Right now, let's talk about the rules from start to finish. This way, whenever one of your readers has a question, he can find it in this chapter of our book."

"Good thinking."

"As usual, I'll start at the beginning."

THE OBJECT OF THE GAME

To win, you have to know where the finish line is and how to get there. The "finish line" in the Monopoly game is reached when all players are bankrupt, save one. That player wins. Pure and simple.

The game is not designed to make all players rich, just one—the winner. Everybody else loses everything.

If you keep the object in mind, you'll see later why so many "house rules" conflict with this goal, because they stretch out the game, making it more of a social exercise than a clear, winner-takes-all competition. Me, I'm a competitive sort. I like the object of this game and the rules as intended.

So now that you know about the finish line, let's talk about what you need to know to run the race.

EQUIPMENT

The Monopoly game has plenty of equipment. I think that's what attracts young players to it in the first place; the excitement of the game is what holds their interest for a lifetime.

There are little, symbolic playing tokens. Nine silver tokens come with the regular game, eleven brass tokens in the "Anniversary" edition, and special gold-tone tokens typically come inside deluxe commemorative editions.

This means up to eleven players can play. But the Monopoly game is best played

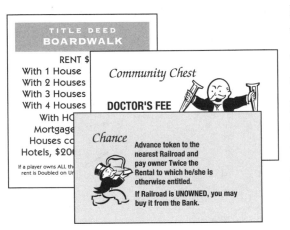

by four or five players. When more play, those who move their token after the first four or five players have the odds stacked against them— there isn't much unsold property on the board ahead by the time their turns come around.

To start any game, appoint a Banker. This person should have a good attention span, because he or she will be kept busy. The Banker needs to count out the Title Deed cards. There should be twenty-eight in all. It helps to arrange them by color-group before play begins. There are sixteen Chance and Community Chest cards. They're shuffled and placed face down on the board. You might keep in mind that, during play, they are not reshuffled. As each card is drawn, it is read, then placed facedown at the bottom of its stack.

There's plenty of money in the Monopoly game. Each player gets $1500 at the start: five each of $1's, $5's, and $10's; six $20's; and two each

of $50's, $100's, and $500's. The rest of the money goes into the Bank, where the Banker watches it like a hawk.

Now comes a very important step: The Banker counts the number of houses and hotels. A game uses exactly thirty-two houses and twelve hotels. (Chances are your set contains an extra one or two—that's

because Parker Brothers wants to make sure you have enough). If you have extras, put them aside and don't use them in play. The official quantities were carefully set, thanks to all those years of "playtesting" back in the twenties and thirties.

STARTING PLAY

Each player selects a token. If there's a conflict, and two or more players want the same token, have each roll the dice. High throw gets to choose.

Now every player rolls both dice to see who moves first. The player who throws the highest amount on both dice gets to move first. Play passes to that player's left (not necessarily the player who threw the second-highest total). Upon completing a turn, the dice are always passed to the player on

the left of the player who just completed his turn. (In the Monopoly game there is no moving out of order, as turns are never lost.)

BUYING PROPERTY

Okay. You've rolled and landed on a piece of property. Let's say you are the first player to land on Oriental Avenue. No one owns it, of course, so you can buy it from the Bank. You pay the Banker its price: $100.

He puts the money in the Bank and gives you the deed to Oriental. Congratulations, you're a property owner.

But what if you don't want to buy it?

AUCTIONS

A good Banker knows how to run a good auction. He is obligated to auction any unowned property as soon as a player landing on it declines to buy it. (As you'll see in a later chapter, it's generally not a good idea to pass up the chance to buy property, but sometimes you just can't afford to buy one you land on.)

The auction begins at whatever price any player is willing to bid. There is no sequence, so players can bid at will, as long as their bid is higher than the last. (Bids must be at least one dollar higher, but usually increments of five or ten dollars more are preferable.)

The Banker encourages the bidding until there are no higher bids. Then he or she announces something like, "I have $90 for Oriental. Ninety dollars. Are there any higher bids? Going . . . Going . . . Gone. Sold to Susan for $90." If anyone wishes to enter a higher bid, he or she would have to shout it our before the Banker says "Gone!"

Can you name this character?

(It's Jake the Jailbird!)

If so, the Banker would start the sequence over. Once a bid is made, it can't be retracted. When you open your mouth, your words are your contract.

PAYING RENT

The payoff for property ownership comes from collecting rent money from an opponent when he lands on its space. The Title Deed for each property lists how much is owed.

When you notice an opponent's token landing on one of your properties, check the Title Deed and announce how much he or she must pay you. Play should pause until you've collected your rent. Notice that rents increase with every house you build on your property, but houses cannot be erected until you own all the properties of the same color. Collectively, these same-colored Title Deeds are called a "color-group."

There are two instances when you cannot collect rent.

The first is because you previously mortgaged the property. Mortgaged property is "inactive" property. We'll talk about mortgaging later.

The second instance is when you forget to ask for rent due you (and the affected opponent hasn't volunteered to pay you). You see, in the Monopoly game, you have to be on your toes. An opponent need not pay a rent unless you ask him or her for it. There is a precise amount of time you have to ask a player to pay rent. Namely, you must ask for it before the second player to his left rolls the dice. In other words, say you're thinking hard about a trade you want to propose. While your concentration is diverted from the board, a player lands on Oriental Avenue, which you own. You're still concentrating as the player to his left rolls the dice and moves. He completes his turn and passes the dice to his left. You finish your thinking and look up. There's the Hat token sitting on Oriental. Wait a moment—that's your property!

Can you still collect your rent?

You can *if* the second player to the left of the Hat hasn't actually rolled the dice yet. If they are still in his hand you can interrupt play and demand your rent money. But if the dice are in the air, or on the board, tough luck! Your opponent is off the hook. Better watch the game more closely from now on.

CHANCE AND COMMUNITY CHEST CARDS

Besides the luck of the dice, the other source of suspense in the Monopoly game lies within the two decks of cards—Chance and Community Chest. They're filled with surprises. Some cards move you to specified spaces. Others give or take money from you. Some require you to go to Jail, while others

give you a chance to get out of Jail without paying $50. Only the last type mentioned may be kept until used. All others are read, acted upon when drawn, and returned facedown to the bottom of the correct deck. These decks are never shuffled during play.

If you have a good memory, when you see the first card of either of these decks reappear, you can make a fairly accurate guess of how many times the dice have been rolled. The probable total is 200 to 250 times. This is because in an average game, it takes about that many moves, among all players, to land on Chance and Community Chest sixteen times each (there are sixteen cards in each deck).

Here are some pointers on the meaning of these cards:

1. Unless specified, any money you must pay goes into the Bank, *not* to Free Parking.

A favorite house rule permits money otherwise owed the Bank to accumulate under the Free Parking corner of the board. The next player to land there collects the total. While this is a nice surprise for the lucky player, this house rule is counterproductive because it makes the game take longer to play. Why? Because the more money in play, the longer it takes to bankrupt all players save one. And the Monopoly game is not a quick game to begin with. But take it from me, a complete game, played by the rules, can be over in two hours or less.

2. If your card directs you to land on GO, you collect your $200. You do not collect again when you move off GO.

3. Many cards advance you to another property. If you pass GO on the way, collect your $200. If the property is already owned, pay the owner the rent due. If the property is unowned, you may buy it from the Bank, or ask the Banker to auction it if you don't wish to buy it.

4. If you roll the dice and move your token past GO on your way to landing on either Chance or Community Chest, you are entitled to your $200 before you draw and read the card. (So if you draw a GO TO JAIL card, for example, you do not lose your $200 because you have already passed GO.)

5. If you draw a Chance card reading ADVANCE TOKEN TO THE NEAREST UTILITY, you move forward to whichever lies closer, the Electric Company or Water Works. If it is unowned, you may buy it. If an opponent already owns it, you must roll the dice again and pay the owner *ten* times the amount thrown.

> *This is different from the usual rule for paying rent on a utility. Usually, you pay based on the throw of the dice that moved your token to the utility. Example: you threw a six to land on Water Works. You would pay the owner $4 × 6 = $24, unless he owned the Electric Company as well, in which case the rent is $10 × 6 = $60.*

6. If you draw a Chance card reading ADVANCE TOKEN TO THE NEAREST RAILROAD, you again move your token to the closest railroad in front of your position on the board. If it is unowned, you may buy it from the Bank. If it is owned, you pay the normal rent.

7. Later in the game, the most costly Chance and Community Chest cards are those requiring money to be paid to the Bank for REPAIRS on houses and hotels you may own.

These cards can cost you dearly. If you have the bad fortune of drawing one, count up your houses and hotels and pay the amount required.

Note: should you have to sell houses or hotels back to the Bank to pay for these costly repairs, you still have to pay based on how many houses/hotels you had before selling some back to raise the money you need. (Talk about a double whammy!)

8. The GET OUT OF JAIL FREE cards are good to have. If you draw one, or collect one in a trade or rent collection, keep it face up near you, next to the board. You may use it whenever you are in Jail and want to leave without paying $50. You don't have to use one if you have it. It is up to you. Note: whenever you need to total your assets, these cards have no monetary value. If you go bankrupt, the player bankrupting you gets any GET OUT OF JAIL FREE cards you may own.

Keep in mind that you should never pay more than $50 to buy one of these cards from another player. After all, this card can only save you $50.

INCOME TAX

Ouch! Another nasty space to land on. When your token has the misfortune of landing on Income Tax you must make a choice. Either pay $200 tax *or* total your assets and pay 10%. Paying the $200 is simple, but you may save money by paying 10%. Warning: if you elect to pay 10%, you can't change your mind once you start to count your assets, even if after totaling your assets you find they total more than $2000. Once you decide to pay 10%, you must pay 10%. Also, if you passed GO on your way to Income Tax, you must include the $200 the Banker paid you before totaling your assets.

Since you started with $1500 in cash, it is unlikely you'll have $2000 or more until the third time you pass GO. On average, you make about $175 every time you go around the board ($200 for passing GO plus some added money due to rents collected and Chance and Community Chest cards drawn, less money taken away by those cards, rents paid, and Luxury Tax. Thus, you should probably pay 10% on your first and second time around the board. Of course, late in the game if you've paid some whopping rents and your assets are low, you should pay 10% instead of $200.

JAIL

The rules require you to go to Jail whenever you 1) land on the GO TO JAIL space, 2) draw a GO TO JAIL card, or 3) roll doubles for the third time on the same turn.

When you go to Jail, you move backwards to the Jail space. You do not collect $200 if you move back past GO. Once in Jail, your turn ends. (No, even if your last throw was doubles, you don't roll again.)

You can get out of Jail by 1) paying $50 before rolling on any of your next three turns, 2) rolling doubles on any of your next three turns, or 3) playing a GET OUT OF JAIL FREE card (which

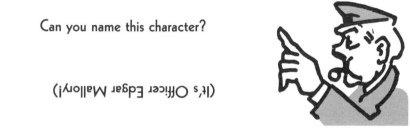

Can you name this character?

(It's Officer Edgar Mallory!)

may be gotten via a trade or already owned). If you do not leave Jail by your third roll, you *must* pay $50 and then move forward according to the total showing on the dice. If you leave Jail by rolling doubles (and not by paying $50), you move out of Jail according to the doubles thrown, but you do not throw again (unlike other instances when doubles are thrown). If you pay $50 or play a GET OUT OF JAIL FREE card before rolling, you may throw again if you roll doubles.

Contrary to some house rules, you still collect rents due you while spending time in Jail.

FREE PARKING

Nothing special happens on this space. It is just a resting place. However, Free Parking is halfway around the board and there is some significance to its location that will be explained in Chapter 4, "The Winning Touch."

HOUSES

Whenever you own an entire color-group you may build houses on those properties.

You may buy houses at any time during your turn. You may also buy houses between the turns of other players. This means after an opponent completes his turn but before the next opponent rolls the

dice to start his turn. (If an opponent rolls a double, it is still his turn and you cannot barge in and buy houses until his complete turn has ended.)

Each Title Deed specifies the cost of building each house on its space. You pay the Bank for each house purchased. The Banker gives you the little green building, which you place on the colored band at the top of the property's space. (When you build the fourth house per property, you'll have to adjust the buildings somewhat to make them all fit.) The rules require you to build "evenly" among the properties of a color-group. This means you can only place one additional house on a property beyond the amount of houses you have on all other properties of the same color-group.

For example, say you own Kentucky, Indiana, and Illinois:

- Your first house may be built on any one of these three properties.
- Your second house must be built on either of the other two properties.

- Your third house must be built on the remaining property.
- Your fourth house may be built on any one of the three properties.
- Your fifth house must be built on either of the properties with one house (not the one with two).
- Your sixth house must be built on the property with just one house erected.

Later in the game, if you are forced to sell houses back to the Bank, you must sell them back "evenly," following this rule in reverse. When you sell houses back to the Bank, you receive one-half their normal cost, according to the Title Deed card of the property where each is located.

Common courtesy dictates that, once you make it clear you wish to buy houses between turns of your opponents, the next player delays throwing the dice until you have a chance to do so.

You'll note that each house increases the rent you collect whenever an opponent lands on your property. But you'll also note that you collect double the basic rent for any property in a monopoly without houses on it ("unimproved property"). For example, if Illinois has a house, but Indiana and/or Kentucky doesn't, you're entitled to double the basic rent on Indiana if it is landed on ($36 instead of $18).

HOTELS

After each property of a color-group has four houses built on it, you may begin building hotels, exchanging the four houses on a property for a hotel piece and paying the Bank its cost. Like the Title Deeds say: hotels equal "four houses plus the cost of a hotel."

You may also break hotels down into houses if you need to raise money, as will be explained.

BUILDING SHORTAGES

Building shortages play a key role in a game played by smart players. Put simply, if the Bank has no houses, you can't buy any. You'll remember that there are exactly thirty-two houses and twelve hotels in a proper Monopoly game set.

This has great importance if you want to build hotels, because if you do not physically have four houses on each property of a color-group—or the houses required to reach a total of four per lot are not available in the Bank—you *cannot* buy and build hotels.

Say you've just acquired the red color-group and there are plenty of hotels in the Bank, but just three houses. It doesn't matter if you have enough money to buy the equivalent of four houses and a hotel for each property in the color-group; all you can buy are those three little green houses!

Not only that, but if you owe a big rent and in order to raise cash you need to sell hotels, you can only replace them with whatever houses remain in the Bank.

Say you have hotels on Kentucky, Indiana, and Illinois and you need to raise $75. You'd like to sell one hotel and exchange it for four houses. But lo and behold, there are only three houses in the Bank. Wow! What a bad break. You must sell all three of your hotels and replace them with those three green houses, collecting half the value of the "houses" sold back to the Bank. Since each hotel is the equivalent of five houses, you were forced to sell the equivalent of four houses from each property in this example. Thus, to raise the needed $75, you were forced to sell your hotels for $900 plus three houses. It cost you $2250 to buy those hotels, so that $75 debt cost you $2250 − $900 plus three $150 houses or a whopping $900! ($2250 − $1350 = $900!)

As I said, housing shortages play a big role in many a game.

Whenever there is more demand for houses in the Bank than there are houses, the Banker has to auction them off one by one. The auction begins with the value of the house for the "cheapest" color-group where a bidder states he will place it if successful in the auction. Let's say that there are three houses left in the Bank. You want to buy them all and build them on the Red color-group, but an opponent wishes them for the Light Blue color-group. The Banker must hold an auction. He sells each one at a time, starting at $50 (the value of a house on the Light Blue color-group). A player who buys a house at auction must place it on the color-group he specified before the auction began.

Note: no matter what price was paid for a house or hotel at auction, it can only be sold back to the Bank for half its stated value on the appropriate Title Deed card!

Houses and hotels can never be sold to another player. So if you make a trade involving an "improved" color-group, you must first sell any houses or hotels on that color-group back to the Bank and collect half their value. Then you can trade the Title Deeds.

On average, you make about $175 every time you go around the board.

MORTGAGES

You can "mortgage" any unimproved property you own at any time. To do so, you turn over its Title Deed and collect its printed mortgage value from the Bank. You can also mortgage improved property, but only after selling back to the Bank all houses and hotels on the color-group.

Once mortgaged, you can no longer collect rent on that property. And when you decide to unmortgage the property, you must repay the Bank the amount of the mortgage plus 10% interest. For example, to unmortgage Park Place, you'd pay the Bank $193 ($175 for the mortgage plus $18 for the interest).

You can sell or trade mortgaged property to any other player. But the acquiring player must either repay the mortgage and 10% interest, or keep the property mortgaged and pay just the 10% interest penalty. However, if that player later "lifts" the mortgage on a future turn, he must pay the 10% interest once more!

BANKRUPTCY

Every player's goal is to avoid bankruptcy. But only one player can win the game. And that means that all other players must first go bankrupt.

In 2007, the *Speed Die* was added to the Monopoly game and its new *Mega* edition. A complete game can now be played in 90 minutes or less!

You're bankrupt if you owe the Bank, or another player, more cash than you can raise and pay. If you can't pay a debt, or make a deal to cover a debt, you are bankrupt.

If it is the Bank you owe money to, you might not be bankrupt. See if you can pay your debt by selling your houses back to the Bank for half price, and/or by mortgaging all of your remaining properties—or by making a trade to raise enough cash to pay your debt. (You are not allowed to make such a deal *unless* you can pay the Bank in full.) If after so doing, your total debt to the Bank

is *not* paid, you are bankrupt. Return all of your Title Deeds to the Bank and any cash you have. The Banker then auctions off each Title Deed you turned in. Each Deed is sold face up as an unmortgaged property (even if mortgaged when you were forced to return it to the Bank). Should you have a GET OUT OF JAIL FREE card, return it to the bottom of the corresponding deck.

Should you go bankrupt to another player, you sell your houses and hotels to the Bank for half price. You then give your cash and Title Deeds to the player you went bankrupt to. If some of those properties are mortgaged, he must pay 10% interest on each even if he doesn't lift the mortgage. He also receives any GET OUT OF JAIL FREE cards you may own.

To avoid bankruptcy, you may try to make a deal with another player, including the one you owe the money to. But if you can't raise enough to cover your debt, you cannot make the deal. You must declare bankruptcy and turn over your assets as described above.

TRADING

While not elaborated upon in the Parker Brothers rules, trading is not only possible in the game; it is vital to the success of the game. You may complete deals with players either on your turn, or in between the turns of other players. As noted, you can't trade houses or hotels. You may only trade Title Deeds, cash, and GET OUT OF JAIL FREE cards. Please let this sink in. You can't trade anything else, like "immunity" from paying rent if a traded property is landed on, or a promise not to build houses, etc. Again, this ruling is designed to assure a reasonable playing time for the game.

The only way you can raise money without making a trade is by mortgaging property or selling houses and hotels back to the Bank.

Players are not permitted to loan money to one another.

This is a game, and games have an advantage over real life because they have rules you can depend upon. If you follow the rules as described above, you'll not only avoid uncertainty and disputes, but you'll be prepared to play any player from anywhere else in the world who follows the official rules. In other words, you too could compete in and win a Monopoly tournament. We'll talk more about tournaments later.

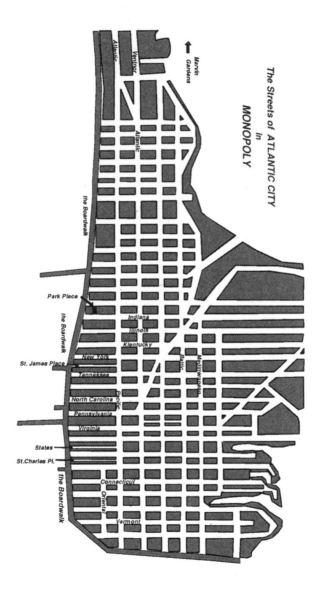

The Streets of ATLANTIC CITY
in
MONOPOLY

A RIDE IN THE RUNABOUT

Armed with the explanation of Monopoly's rules, I accepted Mr. Monopoly's invitation to go for a ride.

We were on Atlantic Avenue now, traveling north. Mr. Monopoly was behind the wheel of his 1935 Cadillac convertible with me seated beside him, taking notes. We entered Atlantic City and he said to me, "A few years back, you'd be staring across that large plaza as a tall, yellow-brick building rose, its style clearly art deco."

Mr. Monopoly pulled to the curb. We stepped out of his car and walked into the plaza. Mr. Monopoly motioned for me to sit beside him on a worn bench.

"Any tour of Atlantic City and the Monopoly board has to begin here. Because the building that used to be here was the main train station in town. Son, those were the days when the Pennsy and the Reading ran their crack passenger runs back and forth from Philadelphia and that building. Both railroads had merged their seashore lines before this building was erected in 1934. So the friendly competition was over by the time the Monopoly game got going."

"That means Darrow didn't arrive at that terminal when he took the train to Atlantic City?"

"Correct. He probably arrived at the old Reading Terminal which used to stand at the corner of Atlantic and Arkansas."

"Where is that?" I asked.

"Son, you're sitting on it."

"What?"

"Yes. When they tore the old terminal down, they turned its site into this open plaza. But, on a brighter note, there's a shiny new train terminal not far from here. Once again, you can catch a train in Philly and be here in under an hour."

"What about the B&O and the Short Line, where did they arrive?"

A skeptical look consumed his face. "The B&O never came to Atlantic City, and the Short Line was a contraction of the Shore Fast Line company. But there was, indeed, a third railroad that used to roar into here. It was the Jersey Central, famous for trains like the Blue Comet which ran here from New York City."

"Another fact Darrow got wrong?"

"Oh well, I guess Charlie never checked. I hear about this goof all the time from train buffs."

But Mr. Monopoly had not taken me here just to discuss a little-known error; he wanted me to see a reminder of the way the city used to be, before showing me the city of today. Looking around, I was saddened to realize the charm of the "World's

Playground" had diminished since 1935. Now it was a gambler's mecca.

We got out of the Cadillac and sat on a bench beneath a poplar tree. The salt air was intoxicating, the traffic nearby a noisy hum.

"In a few minutes I'm going to show you the Atlantic City of today, but it is just as important to know how it was so you can sense the proper dignity of the properties whose names grace the spaces of Monopoly's board. I'm going to tell you a lot about the properties, most importantly which ones are the best ones to own, according to the situation in the game."

"It all starts here. While there's no 'GO' space in the real Atlantic City, that terminal is the best substitute. So imagine we've just rolled the dice and the game has started."

"Okay. I see the dice falling off the top of the bus terminal."

"Good, we move to Baltic and Mediterranean."

We got back in his car and the eye-opening trip around the city began.

I soaked up his narration like a dry sponge. Mr. Monopoly wove tales of the glorious past of the city, its near death in the early seventies, and its renewal following the advent of casino gambling.

After a sumptuous meal at By the Sea, appropriately located at Park Place and the Boardwalk, we strolled the gaily lit Boardwalk before heading back to his home.

Once there, Mr. Monopoly invited me into his library where he proceeded to set up his most elegant version of the Monopoly game—one with a wooden case, brass nameplate, and gold-plated playing pieces.

"We'll relive our experiences today," he said happily, "and I'll give you my opinion about each color-group as I promised. They each have their particular strengths and weaknesses in the game. Your readers can improve their play if they know them."

What followed was the most vivid Monopoly game I ever had the pleasure to play.

"Life is a game," Mr. Monopoly said as we tossed to see who moved first.

Escape maps, compasses, and files were inserted into Monopoly boards smuggled into POW camps inside Germany during World War II. Real money for the escapees was slipped into the packs of Monopoly money!

I pick up the dice. The game begins as I roll a mere three and short-hop my token, the Top Hat, to Baltic Avenue, where ordinary-looking buildings, some rundown, fill my view.

BALTIC AND MEDITERRANEAN—DOGS IN THE GAME, DOGS IN REAL LIFE

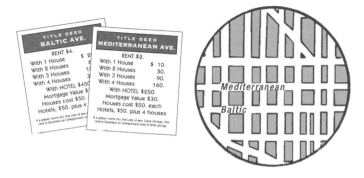

They weren't much in Darrow's time, and they certainly aren't much today. Appropriately, they are the least expensive properties on the board. Each costs only $60.

Both of these avenues wander along the inland side of the city, several blocks from the ocean. Like all the major streets in town, these were arbitrarily titled by a physician named Jonathan Pitney and a famous civil engineer, R. B. Osborne, who surveyed the route the railroads would take to get to the once-deserted island where Atlantic City now stands. Osborne sketched out the street plan for the city. Pitney named the long avenues for great bodies of water—like Atlantic and Pacific, Baltic and Mediterranean—and the cross streets for names of existing states of the union, like Vermont and Connecticut. (The smaller streets not named for states were carved out in later years.) Osborne unknowingly gave the city its name when his plan was finished. He looked down at the newly sketched streets on the northern half of Absecon Island and wondered what to call the new community. The Lenni-Lenape Indians called the island Absegami, which literally meant Little Sea Water. The adjacent sea was anything but little; it was the Atlantic Ocean. Osborne also decided a literal name would suffice, if it had a "ring" to it. So he labeled his town "Atlantic City."

The railroad's investors liked it. A classic name was born.

Even when the city first began, Baltic and Mediterranean were not choice thoroughfares. They simply lay too far from the ocean to be desirable.

As my Top Hat rests on Baltic Avenue, I look around at scores of battered old buildings. I prefer not to linger here.

Mediterranean lies one block further inland. It looks much the same as Baltic. Together, they comprise the city's "backside."

I look down at the deep purple title block: Baltic Avenue. I contemplate its purchase. I recall the words of a realtor Mr. Monopoly knows. We paid his office a visit during the day. "Baltic and Mediterranean are real opportunities," he said confidently. "There's only one way they can go in the future, and that's up."

I know it's almost always best to buy an unowned property. I fork over the paltry $60 to Mr. Monopoly, who is playing Banker. He hands me its deed. I stare down at its rent, a mere $4. I calculate quickly; it will take fifteen rents to recover my little investment. Again I look at the card. Rent with three houses is $180. I must hope to acquire Mediterranean and build houses. Assuming I do get Mediterranean and build a total of six houses, my investment will climb to $420. The $180 rent will repay about 40% of the cash I sank into the ghetto. Three such rents and I'm in the black. Mr. Monopoly asks what's going through my mind as I hand him the dice. I tell him of the math tumbling through my head. He smiles, then reaches into a briefcase and hands me the top two sheets from a folder. "These are my Tip

In the event of a cash shortage, the Bank never runs out of money in Monopoly. The Banker is authorized to act as a temporary "mint," producing extra bills from slips of paper.

Sheets for the Dark Purple group. I've got a set for every other group as well. They're the product of a lifetime of study."

I accept the sheets, noting that they feature nifty charts, with minimal verbiage.

"A picture is worth a thousand words," Mr. Monopoly offers, "It's better to see what the impact of a conclusion is than to have to read it."

ABOUT MR. MONOPOLY'S TIP SHEETS

Mr. Monopoly continued to explain. "You're on the right track by addressing one of the key ideas of property investment in the Monopoly game—figuring the payback of a group when you build on it. There are three other important considerations as well. One is how expensive the monopoly is to develop, a second is how often the property gets landed upon, the third is knowing the time of the game when it can be the most powerful."

- Payback
- Cost
- Frequency
- Power

Mr. Monopoly reiterates all four terms, then gives me an example. "Let's look at Baltic and Mediterranean to see how these concepts apply. First, let's talk about payback. It is obvious the properties are not cost-effective without houses. In fact, until

you have three houses on each, you can't really hope to recover
your investment. That's because of the number of times you'd
need to collect rent to exceed what you've paid to buy the
properties and houses. Take a look on my Tip Sheet. You'll see
that fact on the chart on page 67. If you have only two houses on
each of the Dark Purples, you only get 14 cents back for each
dollar invested when you collect a rent. At that rate, it'll take
seven rents just to break even. But the situation improves when
you build a third house on each; now your average rent jumps to
over 32 cents per dollar. At that rate, only three rents are needed
to break even. And if you buy hotels for each, you make a
whopping 56 cents per dollar per rent. Oh, let me point out that
the 'average rent' on this chart is just that—the average of both
Baltic's and Mediterranean's rents. Since Baltic earns higher
rents, its payback is higher than stated, and Mediterranean earns
a lower rent than printed. I've used the average to represent
the group."

"So hotels on the Dark Purples are a good investment,
right?"

"Yes—and no. True, the second factor—cost—is in your
favor. It costs only $620 to develop the group up to hotels, as
you'll note on the group's cost chart, but now flip to the second
page. You'll see that the third factor—frequency—is not favorable
at all. It so happens that Mediterranean and Baltic are among the
properties landed upon the least."

"Because there are only two properties in the group, or are there other factors as well?"

"Yes, there are events that distort the likelihood of landing on a particular property. Chance and Community Chest, for example. Twelve out of those thirty-two cards send your token to another space. Those spaces have a higher likelihood of being landed on. Most of those passed over have a smaller likelihood. But the major reason is because of Jail. You go to Jail if you land on the corner of the board opposite Jail, if you draw a GO TO JAIL card, or roll doubles for the third time in a turn. Consequently, players frequent Jail several times during an average game. Can you see what this means?"

"It means those spaces that lie beyond Jail get landed on more often, right?"

"Exactly. As it works out, the closer a space is to Free Parking, the more likely it is to be landed on. That ironclad principle is only disturbed by instructions on the Chance and Community Chest cards that send you elsewhere."

"So when we combine these facts, Baltic and Mediterranean get landed on fewer times than other spaces?"

"That's right. Especially since they lie so close to GO. Now the odds of rolling a three like you just did are pretty small. I'll explain the way to calculate dice roll odds later. For now, you only need to know the odds of rolling a three are 2 rolls out of 36, or about 6%. So if your token is located on GO, you will probably not land on Baltic. And since Mediterranean is just one space from GO, you can't possibly land there if your token begins its turn on GO."

"I see what you're saying."

"Finally, there's the question of power. This is the term I use to indicate when a monopoly's average rent exceeds that of any other group. In your case, the question is: how long will Baltic and Mediterranean with hotels maintain their status as the most expensive rents on the gameboard? Take a look at the Power chart. There you'll see that as soon as just one house is built on each of the Reds or Yellows, for example, the Dark Purples have lost their power—their dominance—in the game."

"So this implies that the Dark Purples are a powerful monopoly only very early in the game."

"Exactly—power is a factor of timing. Some monopolies stay in power for a long time, others don't. You'll see this as I give you more of my Tip Sheets."

"Is there any way to sum all this up? You know, to quickly figure out how strong a color-group is?"

"Yes. There's a graph on the second sheet that does just that." I noticed it was called PAYOFF %. "This combines the payback percentage with the odds of landing on the group—the Frequency—and provides an idea of how many cents of rent, per dollar invested, you should expect to collect from each opponent every time he or she makes a complete trip around the board.

Your Dark Purples earn only 14 cents per dollar invested. What does that mean? Since you must invest $620 to own two hotels on this group, it means every time a player completes a trip around the board you should expect to collect $87. If you were facing four opponents, you should earn $348 when they all finish their trips around the board."

"That doesn't strike me as a high return."

"No, as the chart says, this group ranks ninth out of the ten groups."

"So these properties aren't a good buy after all?"

"Take a look at the tip summary on the first sheet. You'll note that they have one potential benefit."

I looked at the sheet. "Creating housing shortages?"

"Precisely. Late in the game, that may be critical to your chances, because it could keep a wealthy opponent from buying hotels to clobber you."

"I see. Well, your sheets seem be a gold mine."

"If used as an aid to making decisions, but not as a substitute. Every game develops differently and you need to adjust accordingly."

"It's good to know there is some value to Baltic and Mediterranean after all."

"Some, but not much. But it's good to know that Baltic and Mediterranean aren't always dogs."

The vision of Baltic fades from my memory as Mr. Monopoly rolls the dice.

MR. MONOPOLY'S TIP SHEETS FOR BALTIC AND MEDITERRANEAN

Each RENT collected on the Dark Purple Group
averages this many cents PAYBACK per dollar invested

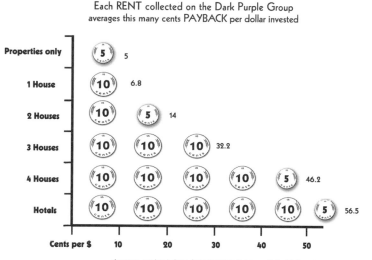

Average payback for a fully developed monopoly is 41.9 cents

The COST to build up the Dark Purple Group

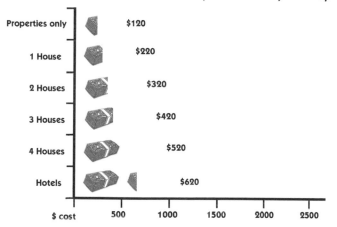

The DARK PURPLE Group with Hotels or 3 Houses...
is the most POWERFUL group if...

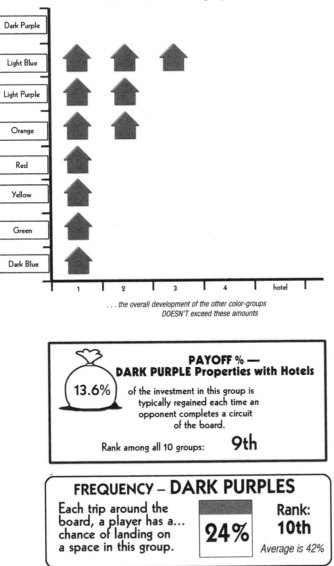

. . . the overall development of the other color-groups
DOESN'T exceed these amounts

PAYOFF % —
DARK PURPLE Properties with Hotels

13.6% of the investment in this group is
typically regained each time an
opponent completes a circuit
of the board.

Rank among all 10 groups: **9th**

FREQUENCY – DARK PURPLES

Each trip around the
board, a player has a...
chance of landing on
a space in this group.

24%

Rank:
10th
Average is 42%

The dice slide across the board and one bounces off the Chance deck. A five and four. The terrier glides to Connecticut Avenue.

ORIENTAL, VERMONT, AND CONNECTICUT— THE LOW-PRICE SPREAD

Connecticut lies near the northern tip of Atlantic City. It runs from the Boardwalk to an inlet called Clam Creek, less than a mile away. I see more modest buildings and the first

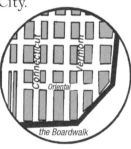

signs of elegance—condos under construction, and casinos in the distance.

Monopoly has to be the biggest builder in America! Who else manufactures a hundred million houses a year?

Connecticut is separated from its less-expensive neighbor, Vermont, by two streets, Rhode Island and Massachusetts. Beyond Vermont lie New Hampshire and Maine. Like the Eastern Seaboard, New England dominates the northern tip of this city's geography.

Oriental is a short avenue running north and south, intersecting all of these streets, ending one block further south at New Jersey. In appearance, it resembles the low-price profile of both Vermont and Connecticut.

Mr. Monopoly buys Connecticut as quickly as a knee responds to the tap of a doctor's hammer. "This is the group I call the low-price spread," he adds as he pays his $120 to the Bank. "If I can buy the other two Light Blues and build quickly, I can usually raise a tidy sum towards building up a more expensive group. Oh yes, here are my Tip Sheets."

MR. MONOPOLY'S TIP SHEETS FOR ORIENTAL, VERMONT AND CONNECTICUT

Each RENT collected on the Light Blue Group
averages this many cents PAYBACK per dollar invested

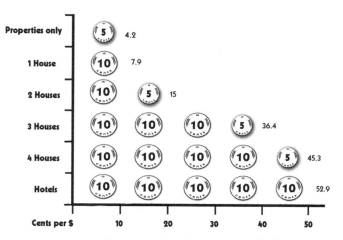

Average payback for a fully developed monopoly is 41.9 cents

The COST to build up the Light Blue Group

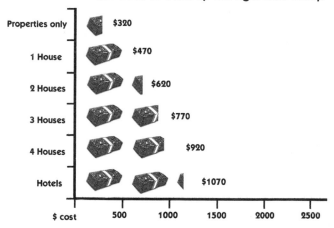

The LIGHT BLUE Group with Hotels or 3 Houses...
is the most POWERFUL group if...

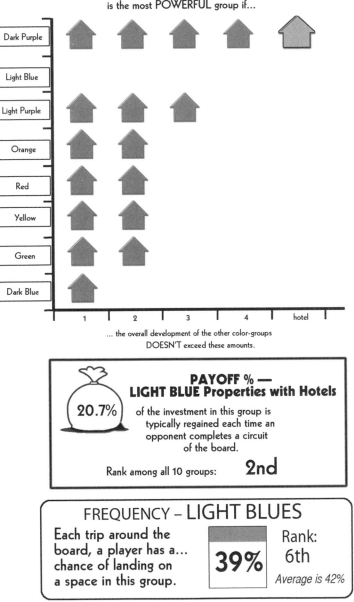

... the overall development of the other color-groups
DOESN'T exceed these amounts.

**PAYOFF % —
LIGHT BLUE Properties with Hotels**

20.7% of the investment in this group is typically regained each time an opponent completes a circuit of the board.

Rank among all 10 groups: **2nd**

FREQUENCY – LIGHT BLUES

Each trip around the board, a player has a... chance of landing on a space in this group.

39%

Rank: 6th

Average is 42%

"I think these properties will prove to be great investments," Mr. Monopoly states as he hands me the dice.

"In the game, or in real life?"

He only smiles in reply as I toss a 6-4 and move the Top Hat to States Avenue.

ST. CHARLES PLACE, STATES, AND VIRGINIA— PROMISE AND PROFIT

I feel unreal; my token rests on a nearly invisible street. Only a nub of States Avenue remains; the remainder is now "under"

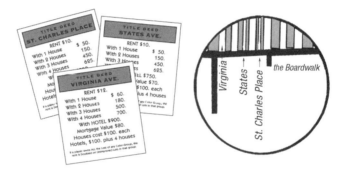

the massive structure of the Showboat Casino Hotel. States was one of a handful of streets that were added after Osborne's plan was adopted. St. Charles is completely gone. It originally bisected a block adjacent to the Boardwalk, separating Delaware from New Jersey Avenue. (States separated Delaware from Maryland Avenue.)

States Avenue was once among the city's prettiest, lined with trees and flowers and pretty homes. Now a most impressive casino rises boldly into the salty air and beckons gamblers from far away to come to Atlantic City in hopes of finding fortune.

Beyond Maryland lies Virginia Avenue, formerly the site of rooming houses where the stars who performed on the Boardwalk would stay. In 1921, the city had 21 theaters and 1000 hotels and rooming houses. Over 100 shows a year opened at famous theaters like the Apollo and Globe. Countless songs were written about the city, perhaps the most famous of which was "By the Sea" by Harry Carroll in 1912. And the famous and nearly famous preferred to stay on Virginia Avenue. Beyond its Boardwalk end, the magnificent Steel Pier jutted 2000 feet into the Atlantic. Among its attractions was the horse and rider who would dive through the air into a pool of water far below.

Virginia today is undergoing renovation along its depleted length. The Steel Pier may be gone, but its memories linger in many an older citizen's heart.

I envision those "better" times; I also envision owning Virginia and St. Charles as I pay $140 for States.

"Good choice," says Mr. Monopoly. "These streets offer promise in real life and profit in the game. They're reasonably priced, get landed on enough, and in tournament play have often decided the winner of the championship round. I hope I land on Virginia," he concludes as he rolls.

"Blast!" Mr. Monopoly mutters as the dice display a 2-1. He moves from Connecticut to the Electric Company and parts with its purchase price, $150.

MR. MONOPOLY'S TIP SHEETS FOR ST. CHARLES, STATES, AND VIRGINIA

Each RENT collected on the Light Purple Group averages this many cents PAYBACK per dollar invested

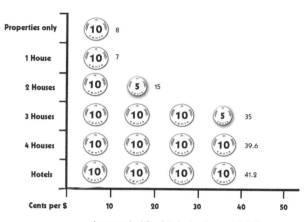

Average payback for a fully developed monopoly is 41.9 cents

The COST to build up the Light Purple Group

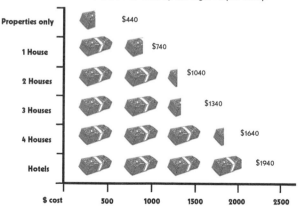

The LIGHT PURPLE Group with Hotels or 3 Houses...
is the most POWERFUL group if...

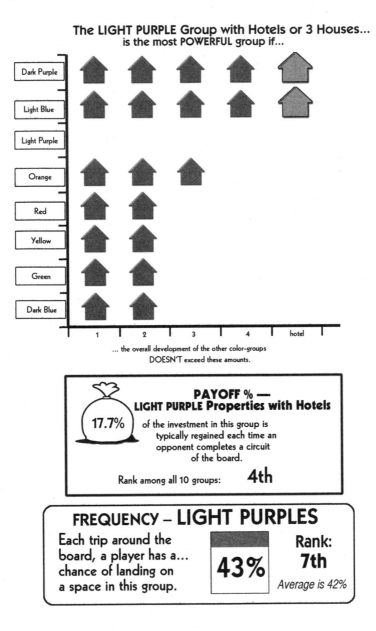

... the overall development of the other color-groups
DOESN'T exceed these amounts.

**PAYOFF % —
LIGHT PURPLE Properties with Hotels**

17.7% of the investment in this group is
typically regained each time an
opponent completes a circuit
of the board.

Rank among all 10 groups: **4th**

FREQUENCY – LIGHT PURPLES

Each trip around the
board, a player has a...
chance of landing on
a space in this group.

43%

**Rank:
7th**

Average is 42%

THE UTILITIES: NOT WHAT THEY SEEM TO BE

There is no Electric Company in Atlantic City anymore. There never was a Water Works. Both are located inland, outside the city.

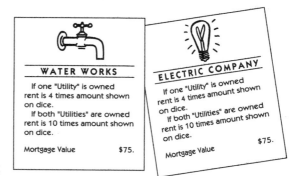

WATER WORKS

If one "Utility" is owned rent is 4 times amount shown on dice.
If both "Utilities" are owned rent is 10 times amount shown on dice.

Mortgage Value $75.

ELECTRIC COMPANY

If one "Utility" is owned rent is 4 times amount shown on dice.
If both "Utilities" are owned rent is 10 times amount shown on dice.
     $75.

Mortgage Value

Pipelines carry fresh water over the salt marshes that separate Atlantic City from the rest of New Jersey. The Electric Company used to be called Atlantic City Electric. Now its territory has expanded, so it has changed its name to Atlantic Electric. Its headquarters moved out of the city in 1982; its main power plant lies several miles south on Great Egg Harbor bay.

I look up at Mr. Monopoly as he adds the Electric Company to his assets. "Don't like the Utilities?" I ask.

"On the contrary," he says to my surprise. "I was just hoping for Virginia. The Utilities aren't as bad as most people think. Sure, you can't build houses on them, but they get landed on throughout the game and produce a lot of cash on a low investment. Many players mortgage them at the drop of a hat. You'll notice I won't do that. Check out my Tip Sheet."

MR. MONOPOLY'S TIP SHEETS FOR THE UTILITIES

Each RENT collected on the Utilities
averages this many cents PAYBACK per dollar invested

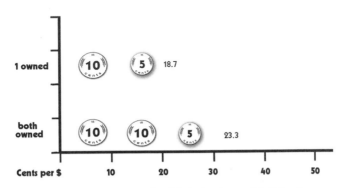

1 owned	18.7
both owned	23.3

Cents per $

Average payback for a fully developed monopoly is 41.9 cents

The COST to own the Utilities

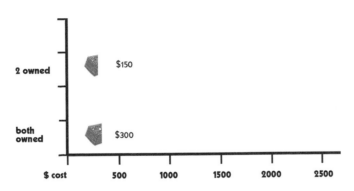

2 owned	$150
both owned	$300

$ cost

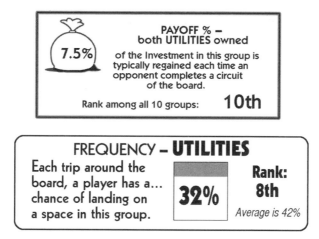

My Top Hat lies in front of Mr. Monopoly's Terrier now. I look forward to all the juicy unsold properties ahead of me. Like a runner in the lead, I lean forward as I throw the dice, as if I can help them attain a higher number.

It works. I throw a nine.

Chance.

I draw the top card in the deck; I must move back three spaces.

"What luck!" Mr. Monopoly utters as I backtrack to New York Avenue. "The best property in the best color-group. If not for the Chance and Community Chest cards, New York would be the most frequently landed-upon property in the game. Only Illinois and the B&O outrank it for frequency."

ST. JAMES PLACE, TENNESSEE, AND NEW YORK—THE SWEET ORANGES

New York lies in the heart of the city, running across the island from the Boardwalk to Huron, the most inland north-south street. Equally long is Tennessee Avenue, two blocks to

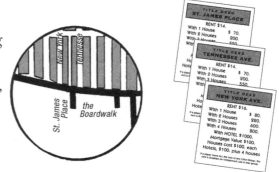

the north and terminating at Central Pier and the Boardwalk. (Several blocks separate these streets from Virginia.) St. James is but a block long, running between New York and Tennessee from the Boardwalk to Pacific. Well-kept rooming houses once populated the shortish street. A few are still open, most notably one whose porch brims with flowers, called the Brunswick, where its elderly owner turned out to greet Mr. Monopoly with hugs and kisses. "She's been here almost as long as I have," Mr. Monopoly explained.

My Top Hat rests on New York, among vacant lots and spotty construction. A young lady dressed in an orange skirt walks down the street; the breeze causes her skirt to dance, as in a play.

"Ah, sweet orange," Mr. Monopoly says with a gleam in his eye.

I realize I am back at the game. I buy New York.

"Personally, I favor the orange properties more than any other group," Mr. Monopoly notes. "They're not too expensive to buy and develop, get landed on a lot—and I do mean a lot—and can knock out many an unlucky player who faces a rent there."

MR. MONOPOLY'S TIP SHEETS FOR ST. JAMES, TENNESSEE, AND NEW YORK

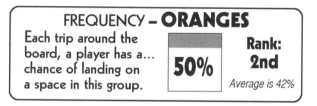

FREQUENCY – **ORANGES**

Each trip around the board, a player has a... chance of landing on a space in this group. **50%**

Rank: **2nd**

Average is 42%

Inflation? Never heard of it. Values on the Monopoly gameboard are the same today as they were in 1935!

Each RENT collected on the Orange Group
averages this many cents PAYBACK per dollar invested

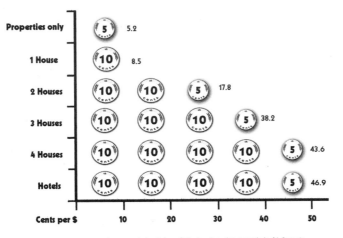

Average payback for a fully developed monopoly is 41.9 cents

The COST to build up the Orange Group

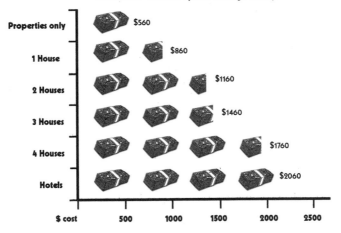

The ORANGE Group with Hotels or 3 Houses...
is the most POWERFUL group if...

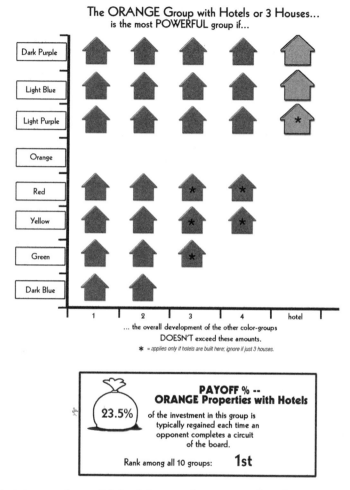

... the overall development of the other color-groups
DOESN'T exceed these amounts.

✱ = applies only if hotels are built here; ignore if just 3 houses.

**PAYOFF % --
ORANGE Properties with Hotels**

23.5%

of the investment in this group is
typically regained each time an
opponent completes a circuit
of the board.

Rank among all 10 groups: **1st**

"Got to catch up," Mr. Monopoly says as he throws a nine. "Ah, very nice."

The Terrier alights on Kentucky.

KENTUCKY, INDIANA, AND ILLINOIS—
THE HEART OF THE TOWN AND THE GAME

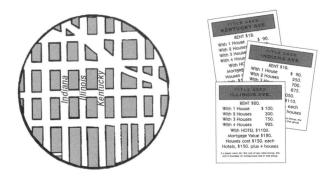

Across the street from the Terrier stands, appropriately, a Kentucky Fried Chicken. Further down I see Clifton's Club Harlem. Other nightlife venues once abounded on Kentucky, according to Mr. Monopoly, but no longer. I try to visualize how it once looked. I can't. The city has changed so much, thanks to casino gambling. Mr. Monopoly reminds me that progress and change are inevitable, just like one's fortunes in the Monopoly game.

Kentucky, Illinois, and Indiana lie, in succession, south of New York. So their sequence on the board makes sense.

One of the great hotels of Atlantic City stood at the corner of Boardwalk and Illinois: the Claridge. This landmark structure was inexorably headed for demolition when casino gambling was legalized in the city. It was refurbished and became a combination hotel and casino.

Not so fortunate was the legendary Brighton, at the corner of Indiana and the Boardwalk. The Brighton was only *the* most exclusive hotel in the city during the 1920s. A common man like Darrow could not afford to stay there. One did not arrive at the Brighton in a motorcar, or for that matter as a passenger on a train. Its guests arrived by way of private railway cars! Many stayed all summer. Today the site is reshaped by the profile of the Sands hotel-casino.

All three of these streets pierce the width of the island. While still depressed, there is a cautious air of optimism about their future. "They've got a great location, near the center of the city," Mr. Monopoly offered. "It's only a matter of time before they make their impact."

And much the same is true of their role in the game. It is only a matter of time before a monopoly on the reds dominates the game. The properties are ideally located in the Monopoly game. Adjacent to Free Parking, enhanced by the ADVANCE TO ILLINOIS AVENUE Chance card, they are visited nearly as frequently as the Oranges. They are more expensive, but when developed they produce "killer" rents.

Mr. Monopoly's tip sheets tell all.

MR. MONOPOLY'S TIP SHEETS FOR KENTUCKY, INDIANA, AND ILLINOIS

Each RENT collected on the Red Group
averages this many cents PAYBACK per dollar invested

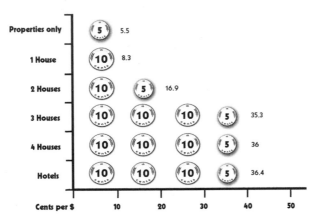

Properties only	5.5
1 House	8.3
2 Houses	16.9
3 Houses	35.3
4 Houses	36
Hotels	36.4

Cents per $ 10   20   30   40   50

Average payback for a fully developed monopoly is 41.9 cents

The COST to build up the Red Group

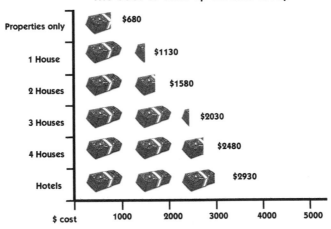

Properties only	$680
1 House	$1130
2 Houses	$1580
3 Houses	$2030
4 Houses	$2480
Hotels	$2930

$ cost   1000   2000   3000   4000   5000

The RED Group with Hotels or 3 Houses...
is the most POWERFUL group if...

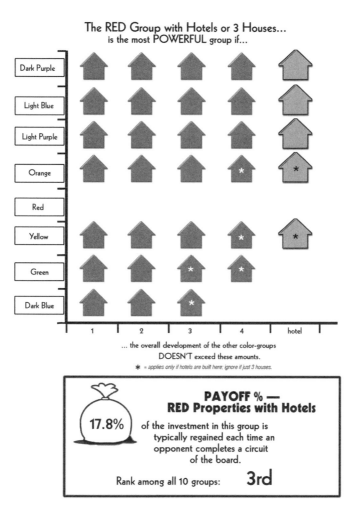

... the overall development of the other color-groups
DOESN'T exceed these amounts.

✱ = applies only if hotels are built here; ignore if just 3 houses.

**PAYOFF % —
RED Properties with Hotels**

17.8% of the investment in this group is
typically regained each time an
opponent completes a circuit
of the board.

Rank among all 10 groups: **3rd**

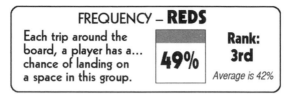

Mr. Monopoly finishes purchasing Kentucky; I roll again. My luck changes.

Eleven.

Go to Jail.

I backtrack my token twenty spaces, and place the Top Hat on the picture of Jake the Jailbird, peering through the bars.

There is a jail in Atlantic City, although it is more often referred to as a holding facility. Criminals of all types are detained here until sent elsewhere, depending on their crime. Like most jails, this one looks cold, unfriendly, and dreary.

I am glad my sentence is a maximum of three rolls of the dice.

Mr. Monopoly tries to suppress a gleeful laugh. He rolls a five and the laugh spills out. It is a laugh of sheer delight.

He has landed on Ventnor Avenue and gladly pays $260 to buy it.

ATLANTIC, VENTNOR, AND MARVIN GARDENS—UP AND OUT OF TOWN

The Terrier eyes the pet shop on Ventnor Avenue. There are many stores on this street. Curiously, Ventnor becomes Atlantic Avenue

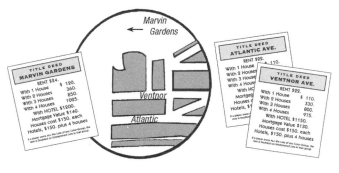

just after leaving Atlantic City. At the intersection where the names change, Atlantic Avenue veers east at a fork in the road and joins Pacific Avenue. (Sounds confusing, yes?) Lo and behold, Pacific then yields its name to Atlantic Avenue, which—like Ventnor—runs south for the entire course of Absecon Avenue through the communities of Ventnor, Margate, and Longport.

The eventual 1975 Monopoly champion, John Mair of Ireland, boasted that the deciding match turned in his favor when he inadvertently dropped his dice into his beer glass instead of into the dice cup provided. Why was this mistake to his advantage? "I had to move on to gin and tonic," he explained.

Ventnor Avenue is dotted with professional offices—doctors and the like—and pretty trees and hydrangeas, the city's official flower. Here, due to the salty climate, they bloom pink, not blue or white.

Marvin Gardens (which we all know should be spelled Marven Gardens) is the one space that is not a street but a carefully planned redoubt nestled inside the town of Margate, south of Atlantic City proper. Its inclusion in the game is wise because its elite status was well established in the 1930s and surely appealing to those who named the spaces on the Monopoly board. There is no similar enclave anywhere else in or near Atlantic City.

Marven Gardens is even patrolled by its own police force. Appropriately, it is adjacent to the Go to Jail space.

The three Yellows are good properties to own. They are slightly more expensive than the reds but do not get landed upon as much, since they are further from Jail and no Chance card sends a token flying to one of these spaces. Their rents, nonetheless, are usually crippling later in the game.

MR. MONOPOLY'S TIP SHEETS FOR ATLANTIC, VENTNOR, AND MARVIN GARDENS

Each RENT collected on the Yellow Group
averages this many cents PAYBACK per dollar invested

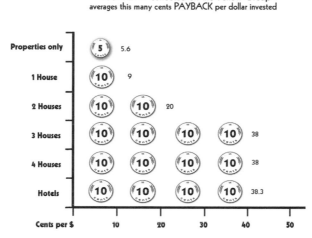

Average payback for a fully developed monopoly is 41.9 cents.

The COST to build up the Yellow Group

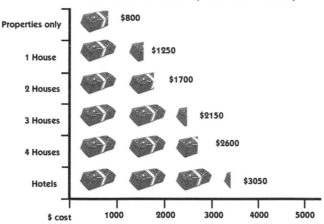

The YELLOW Group with Hotels or 3 Houses...
is the most POWERFUL group if...

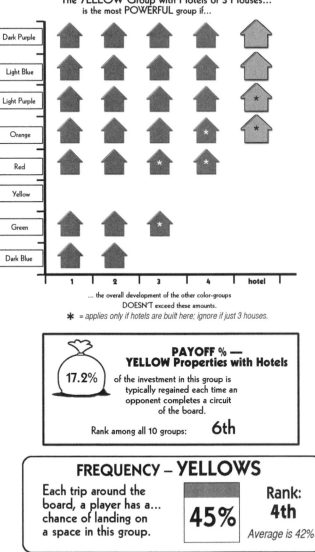

... the overall development of the other color-groups
DOESN'T exceed these amounts.

✱ = applies only if hotels are built here; ignore if just 3 houses.

**PAYOFF % —
YELLOW Properties with Hotels**

17.2% of the investment in this group is typically regained each time an opponent completes a circuit of the board.

Rank among all 10 groups: **6th**

FREQUENCY – YELLOWS

Each trip around the board, a player has a... chance of landing on a space in this group.

45%

Rank: **4th**

Average is 42%

I look out from the cell I occupy. Absent-mindedly, I throw the dice. "You should have paid," Mr. Monopoly reminds me as a seven stares me in the face. I feel foolish. Early in the game you need to be in motion around the board to accumulate property. Sitting in Jail does one no good at this stage.

Mr. Monopoly throws the first doubles. Two threes. He bounces to Community Chest and draws a card.

Years ago, Community Chest was the forerunner of the United Way. As a civic fund-raising organization it helped the unfortunate. The space Mr. Monopoly's token rests neatly upon is adjacent to Pacific Avenue. (The real Community Chest building was also located on Pacific Avenue.)

Mr. Monopoly draws the YOU HAVE WON SECOND PRIZE IN A BEAUTY CONTEST card. He chortles as he collects the $10 prize.

The Miss America pageant was held each year in the huge Convention Center at Boardwalk and Mississippi. It is big enough to play football games inside. Helicopters have flown around its spacious interior. Presidents have been nominated from its floor. It was built in 1929 to bring winter traffic into the city.

In 1987, under its huge arched roof, the second-place winner in the Miss America pageant won $20,000.

Ten dollars richer, Mr. Monopoly picks up his dice and throws doubles again, landing his terrier squarely on Mediterranean, which he buys, blocking my possible monopoly. He is the first to complete a circuit around the board and claims his $200 salary. I watch from Jail as the dice hit the board for the third time. A five and a four. The Terrier is now outside my cell, staring in. "Just visiting!" Mr. Monopoly exclaims. "Glad I didn't roll a third doubles."

I do not chance another roll without paying. After parting with my $50, I exit my cell and roll a five. I am on the platform of the Pennsylvania Railroad.

THE RAILROADS—CASH COWS

It is 1927 and hundreds of people mill about me, waiting for the 6:12 to whisk us back to Philadelphia. Times are good. The ladies are dressed in their finest, and the men wear top hats like Mr. Monopoly. You can breathe the prosperity in the air.

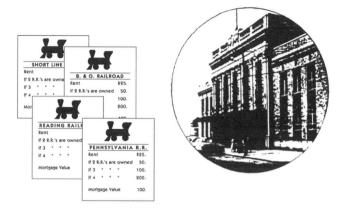

I blink my eyes and the lovely vision Mr. Monopoly just recollected for me gives way to the sight of quiet empty tracks leading out from the city. Far fewer trains arrive these days, but the new high-speed line carries on the tradition. Since 1989, it has whisked people back and forth from Philadelphia and other cities. However, these passengers are mainly day visitors, down to gamble their stakes at the casinos and then head home. I look back at the bus terminal Mr. Monopoly first showed me. I try to imagine the eight pairs of tracks supporting steaming loco-motives, the sheltering roofs above the intervening platforms, the deep red cars of the Pennsy, the green cars of the Reading, the blue ones of the Jersey Central's Blue Comet. My imagination proves insufficient.

I pay $200 and take possession of the first railroad. Inwardly, I am delighted in knowing that the Pennsylvania Railroad still runs in Monopoly (except when it is mortgaged).

"The railroads are a pretty good investment, you know," Mr. Monopoly offers. "You may not get rich on them, but they're a steady source of cash. If you own all four, they're really cash cows. They get landed on frequently, thanks to the two Chance cards that send you to the nearest railroads, plus the TAKE A RIDE ON THE READING card. By the way, a lot of folks mispronounce its name. It isn't the REED-ING Railroad; it's the RED-ING Railroad. Named after the city in Pennsylvania where it was headquartered."

Mr. Monopoly first joined the Monopoly team in 1936.

MR. MONOPOLY'S TIP SHEET FOR THE RAILROADS

Each RENT collected on the RAILROADS
averages this many cents PAYBACK per dollar invested

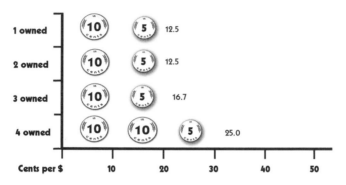

Average payback for a fully developed monopoly is 41.9 cents.

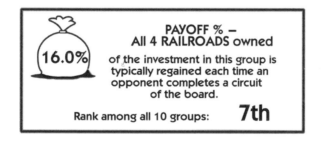

PAYOFF % –
All 4 RAILROADS owned

16.0% of the investment in this group is typically regained each time an opponent completes a circuit of the board.

Rank among all 10 groups: **7th**

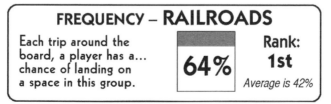

FREQUENCY – RAILROADS

Each trip around the board, a player has a... chance of landing on a space in this group.

64%

Rank: **1st**

Average is 42%

The COST to own the Railroads

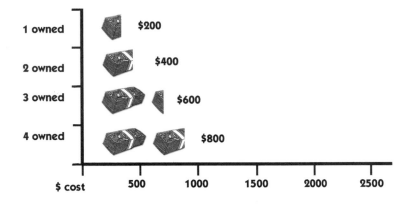

1 owned	$200
2 owned	$400
3 owned	$600
4 owned	$800

$ cost   500   1000   1500   2000   2500

Mr. Monopoly continues to move by leaps and bounds. Another doubles advances him to Free Parking. "Ho! If there's one thing you won't find in Atlantic City today, it is free parking. The casinos attract so many visitors, the employees have to park their cars along the Atlantic City Expressway, miles outside of town. The casinos bus them in from there. A lot of buildings were torn down to create parking lots that charge a king's ransom. Back in Darrow's time, things weren't so dear and not all streets in the city were lined with parking meters and their hand-cranked, orange 'Violation' wheels."

Again he throws. The Terrier is off again. This time twelve spaces fly under its feet until it comes to rest on the green of North Carolina. At age 22, John Philip Sousa performed in public for the first time at North Carolina and the Boardwalk, at the Haddon Hall—another of the city's great old hotels. Today, mercifully, it still exists as a hotel-casino.

PACIFIC, NORTH CAROLINA, AND PENNSYLVANIA—FOR THE EXPENSIVE TASTES

After a fairly orderly progression southward, North Carolina and Pennsylvania break the pattern of naming streets around the board. They are located between Tennessee and Virginia—properties on the opposite side of the gameboard. Pacific intersects both, and most of the other cross-streets in town. The decision to place them on the prestigious fourth side of

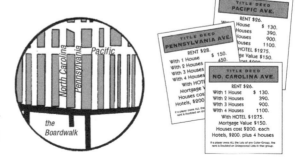

the board has merit. They were elite streets in the twenties and thirties; they held their ground in the decay of the sixties and the seventies. Today, both streets terminate astride the first casino in Atlantic City—and the heart of the Boardwalk's attractions.

"The Greens are my least favorite group. They're for those whose taste runs expensive—in the game, that is." Mr. Monopoly speaks while contemplating the $300 cost of buying the property. "They lie just beyond GO TO JAIL and don't get landed on as much as the properties on the prior two sides of the board. They're awfully expensive, so you can't afford to develop them early. And they don't pay back, dollar for dollar, as quickly as most properties."

"Are you going to auction it?" I ask as he stares at my holdings.

"No," he says crisply as he places the bills in the Bank. They can dominate if the game goes a long while." He studies the board and eyes my holdings. I wonder what he's thinking.

MR. MONOPOLY'S TIP SHEETS FOR PACIFIC, NORTH CAROLINA, AND PENNSYLVANIA

Each RENT collected on the Green Group averages this many cents PAYBACK per dollar invested

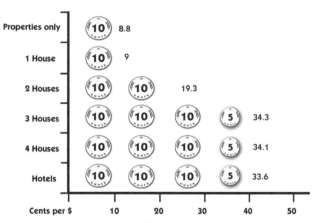

Average payback for a fully developed monopoly is 41.9 cents.

The COST to build up the Green Group

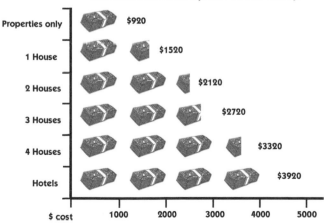

The GREEN Group with Hotels or 3 Houses...
is the most POWERFUL group if...

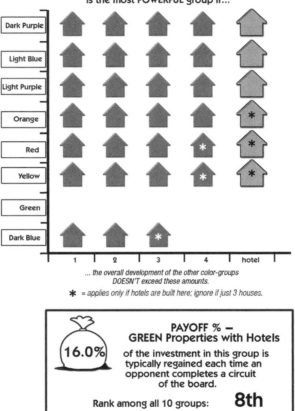

... the overall development of the other color-groups
DOESN'T exceed these amounts.

✱ = applies only if hotels are built here; ignore if just 3 houses.

PAYOFF % —
GREEN Properties with Hotels

16.0% of the investment in this group is typically regained each time an opponent completes a circuit of the board.

Rank among all 10 groups: **8th**

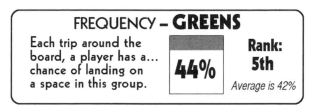

Mr. Monopoly rolls yet again. Finally, his luck changes as he lands on Luxury Tax and begrudgingly tosses $75 in the Bank. In the land of the unemployed and the welfare recipient, even Atlantic City has a strip where the wealthy thrive. The tax on luxuries there is evident. Prices are dear. But the "strip" has a famous name and I am destined to land on it.

I roll a seven. Chance. There is no real "chance" in Atlantic City, except possibly in the casinos.

I draw, then smile. I am told to advance my Top Hat to Boardwalk.

BOARDWALK AND PARK PLACE—THE DOMAIN OF THE RICH AND FAMOUS

The Boardwalk was begun for practical reasons. In the mid-1800s, a hotel owner named Alexander Boardman suggested to his peers that a walkway of wooden planks be built along the shore to prevent guests from tracking sand into their seaside hotels. The idea made sense; the first boardwalk became a reality.

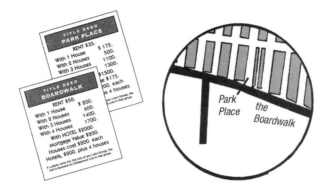

This boardwalk attracted more hotels. The wooden walkway was soon enlarged, then built permanently on concrete piers. In no time, this promenade became the center of life in the city as every visitor was lured to stroll its two-mile length.

In this century, the Boardwalk was further extended through Ventnor, Margate, and Longport, its total length surpassing seven miles. Great piers, like the Steel Pier, were built beyond it over the sea. Among the dazzling variety of attractions built along its length was Lucy, the six-story-tall elephant. She was a gimmick to sell advertising, but in time became first a tavern, then a cottage, and then a restaurant. Today, relocated away from the shore, she is a National Historic Landmark.

The Boardwalk is everything to Atlantic City, and to many players, it is everything to the game. So symbolic is it of grand wealth and fortune that Parker Brothers introduced a new game in Monopoly's fiftieth year called Advance to Boardwalk.

Unlike the grandeur of the Boardwalk, Park Place is tiny by comparison. It is a street, not a park, before the Claridge Hotel between Indiana and Ohio Avenues. There is an adjoining park, named Brighton Park. It is there on the Boardwalk, next to lovely Brighton Park, that a bronze plaque is mounted, featuring the profile of Charles Darrow, commemorating him and the Monopoly game.

Property values are the highest here, both on the board and in the city itself. Only wealthy "players" can afford to own them.

In the game, as Mr. Monopoly informs me, both Park Place and Boardwalk offer high return on investment. Since there are only two properties in this group, it is actually cheaper to develop them than the three-property Green group. While Park Place is not landed on as much as other properties, Boardwalk is landed on more often, thanks to the card that brought me here.

I gladly pay my $400 and add its rich, blue deed to my collection.

MR. MONOPOLY'S TIP SHEETS FOR BOARDWALK AND PARK PLACE

Each RENT collected on the Dark Blue Group averages this many cents PAYBACK per dollar invested

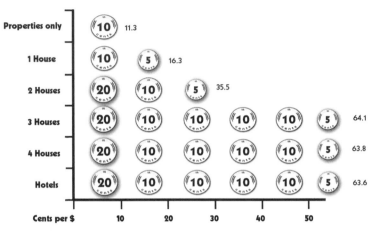

Properties only	10 cents					11.3
1 House	10 cents	5				16.3
2 Houses	20 cents	10 cents	5			35.5
3 Houses	20 cents	10 cents	10 cents	10 cents	10 cents	5 · 64.1
4 Houses	20 cents	10 cents	10 cents	10 cents	10 cents	5 · 63.8
Hotels	20 cents	10 cents	10 cents	10 cents	10 cents	5 · 63.6

Cents per $ 10   20   30   40   50

Average payback for a fully developed monopoly is 41.9 cents.

The COST to build up the Dark Blue Group

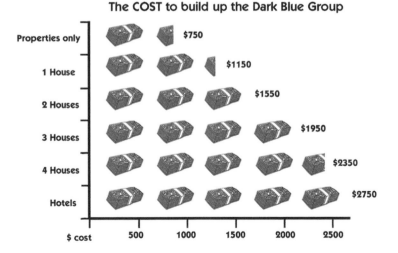

Properties only	$750
1 House	$1150
2 Houses	$1550
3 Houses	$1950
4 Houses	$2350
Hotels	$2750

$ cost   500   1000   1500   2000   2500

The DARK BLUE Group with Hotels or 3 Houses...
is the most POWERFUL group if...

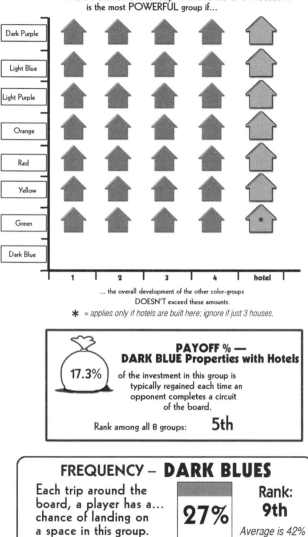

	1	2	3	4	hotel
Dark Purple					
Light Blue					
Light Purple					
Orange					
Red					
Yellow					
Green					
Dark Blue					

... the overall development of the other color-groups
DOESN'T exceed these amounts.

* = applies only if hotels are built here; ignore if just 3 houses.

**PAYOFF % —
DARK BLUE Properties with Hotels**

17.3%

of the investment in this group is typically regained each time an opponent completes a circuit of the board.

Rank among all 8 groups: **5th**

FREQUENCY – **DARK BLUES**

Each trip around the board, a player has a... chance of landing on a space in this group.

27%

Rank: **9th**

Average is 42%

"Well," says Mr. Monopoly, "we're both ready to get serious. We're about to go around the board again and I smell a rent coming."

He picked up the dice and threw an eight. $200 for passing GO plus the deed for Oriental Avenue were soon in his hands.

"So much for history and reminiscing. Now that we're into the game, and I've explained my Tip Sheets, I'm going to offer you my favorite tactics and strategies."

"Ah, Mr. Monopoly's 'Winning Touch'?" I offered.

"Precisely. And they're not long-winded. I keep 'em short and sweet."

I hoped my luck would be just as sweet.

One of the more controversial moments in the 1983 United States Championship Tournament occurred when a player decided to reduce his three hotels to twelve houses in order to block an opponent from buying the remaining houses in the Bank. From this incident forward, this tactic was outlawed in tournament play. The Chief Judge ruled that a building shortage is in effect only if property development is halted at the four house level. By moving up to hotels, a player forgoes his right to "back into" a housing shortage should other players wish to purchase the houses remaining in the Bank.

PROPERTY GROUP SUMMARIES

Group	Max. Cost fully developed	Payback	Frequency	Payoff
Dark Purples	$620	56.5%	24%	13.6%
Light Blues	$1070	52.9%	39%	20.7%
Light Purples	$1940	41.2%	43%	17.7%
Utilities	$300	23.3%	32%	7.5%
Oranges	$2060	46.9%	50%	23.5%
Reds	$2930	36.4%	49%	17.8%
Yellows	$3050	38.3%	45%	17.2%
Railroads	$800	25.0%	64%	16.0%
Greens	$3920	33.6%	44%	16.0%
Dark Blues	$2750	63.6%	27%	17.3%

THE END GAME BEGINS

"The Monopoly game is just like life," Mr. Monopoly said as he surveyed the game we were playing. "There are no hard and fast rules for success, but there are principles that improve your chances. If you learn them and work them to your advantage you'll win more than you lose."

I had finally passed GO, landing on the Reading Railroad, which I purchased with my $200 salary. Mr. Monopoly threw a ten and bought St. James. "Now here's an instance where I can put my principles to work. I'm buying St. James for $180. By so doing, I take away your chance to get all the Orange properties without having to make a deal with me. Since the Oranges are such a productive group, I'd rather not face three imposing hotels there, poised to wipe me out. Unless, of course, I can get a reasonable value in trade from you."

"I can't argue with your logic."

"Good, I just demonstrated two of my principles. The first pertains to blocking an opponent's desired monopoly. The second has to do with trading techniques." Mr. Monopoly did not elaborate. Instead, he dipped into a briefcase and soon handed me more carefully worded sheets of advice. They were titled:

MR. MONOPOLY'S SYSTEM OF WINNING AT THE MONOPOLY GAME

1. NEVER FORGET THE OBJECT OF THE GAME.

The object is to bankrupt all opponents. To do so, you must be dedicated and make each decision with the aim of improving your chances of wiping out your opponents.

Never let an opponent off the ropes. Luck plays a key role in the game and luck can turn against you if you do not bankrupt a player as quickly as you can.

2. KNOW THE EQUIPMENT WELL.

Remember that there are thirty-two houses and twelve hotels. Use this knowledge to create housing shortages when it is to your advantage (more on this later).

There are sixteen Chance Cards.

CHANCE

- Ten of these cards move you elsewhere.
- Two give you money ("rewards").
- Two take money away ("penalties").
- One takes money away if you own buildings.
- One lets you get out of Jail free.

A Chance card will most likely send you to another space.

Keep track of which cards have been played. Since the deck is not shuffled, you can deduce which cards haven't come up. If you have a great memory, you'll know which cards to expect when they recycle.

There are sixteen Community Chest cards.

COMMUNITY CHEST

- Nine of these cards give you money ("rewards").
- Three take money away ("penalties").
- Two move you elsewhere.
- One takes money away if you own buildings.
- One lets you out of Jail free.

A Community Chest card will most likely give you a reward. Keep track of cards played from this deck as well.

The best Monopoly players can predict which Chance and Community Chest cards will be drawn. Because the decks are never shuffled, all a player has to do is memorize the sequence in which the cards first appeared. Though the task is less daunting than it may initially seem—there are only sixteen cards in each deck—it's still quite a trick.

Know the odds of throwing any number with the dice. Study the following chart.

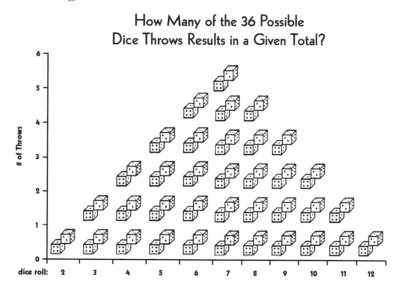

How Many of the 36 Possible Dice Throws Results in a Given Total?

3. KEEP TABS ON THE AMOUNT OF MONEY IN THE GAME.

- Each player starts with $1500.
- On an average circuit of the board, prior to houses appearing, a player will make about $170. (This takes into account passing GO, earning rewards, paying penalties and taxes, and the effect of rents.)
- By knowing approximately how much cash an opponent has, you can know how far he can bid in an auction, or how

much rent he can afford to pay, or how many buildings he can purchase without mortgaging. This knowledge enhances your own decision making.

4. IT USUALLY TAKES FIVE TURNS TO GO AROUND THE BOARD.

- Every time you go around the board, you'll probably roll doubles once, and you'll probably land on four of the twenty-eight property spaces.

- Count how many unmortgaged properties your opponents own and divide by 7. That will tell you how many rents you can expect to pay on your next circuit around the board. Example: your opponents collectively own eleven properties. You can expect to land on 1.6 (round off to 2) of them on your next circuit of the board.

5. YOU SHOULD ALWAYS BUY AN UNOWNED PROPERTY IF . . .

- No other player owns a property in its color-group.
- It gives you a second or third property of its group.
- It blocks an opponent from getting a complete color-group.
- It is an Orange property (always block this group if you can).

Exception:

- Don't feel you must block a group if two other players each have a property of the group and also have more valuable groups split between them.

  Example: Players A and B own all the Reds and Oranges between them. They each own a Light Purple. You land on the unowned Light Purple. You do not need to buy it. Counterexample: Players A and B own all the Oranges and Light Purples between them. They each own a Red. You land on the unowned Red. You *should* buy it. Otherwise you increase the chances these players will trade and develop the most powerful group among the three groups (which is the Reds).

6. KNOW THE PROS AND CONS OF EACH COLOR-GROUP.

- Study the Property Tip Sheets. Know them well.

7. KNOW WHEN TO PAY 10% INCOME TAX.

- Pay 10% if you haven't gone around the board three times. (Remember, you started with $1500 and will probably make $170 each time you go around the board. After three turns your assets should be over $2000.)
- Pay 10% later in the game only if you have paid heavy rents and think your assets are below $1500.

8. **KNOW WHEN TO STAY IN JAIL.**

- Pay $50 and get out of Jail early in the game while many properties remain unowned or undeveloped. You need to be in circulation.
- When most properties are developed between Jail and the Go to Jail space, roll the dice and hope you stay in Jail. This is especially important when some color-groups are heavily developed. By staying in Jail you reduce the chance of landing on such a group before an opponent lands on yours.

9. **KNOW WHEN AND WHERE TO BUILD HOUSES AND HOTELS.**

Building advances your ability to bankrupt your opponents. Many players build all they can afford. Often, this strategy causes losses because houses must be torn down to pay rents or other penalties if sufficient cash or mortgagable properties aren't left in reserve.

You should build when . . .

- You form the first complete color-group.
- You can build and still be left with enough cash to pay a high probability expense: namely, rents on railroads or utilities, Luxury Tax, or the worse Community Chest or Chance cards.
- $150 to $200 is all the cash you need to hold on to if there are no other complete color-groups against you.

- Keep $300 to $400 in cash on hand after building on a color-group beyond Free Parking if there is one or more developed color-groups against you.
- Exception: late in the game, when it is "all or nothing," build all you can if you think you can financially cripple an opponent.

When you build, build according to these tips:
- Build a complete color-group up to at least three houses per property before you start building on a second color-group.
- Rents rise dramatically between having two and three houses per property. See the graph below.

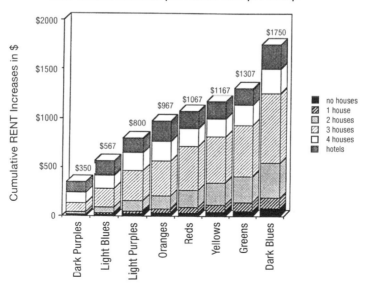

How RENTS Increase per House Built per Group

If you can afford an extra house, put it on the most expensive property of the color-group.

- when buying a second "extra" house for a three-property group, put the second house on the middle property if the group is Light Blue or Orange.
- put the second extra house on the first property if the group is Light Purple, Red, Yellow, or Green.
- Build up to the fourth house or hotel level only if you can truly afford to, except if the group is one of the first three on the board (Dark Purple, Light Blue, Light Purple). Due to the low rents of these groups, you should always try to build hotels here.
- Early in the game, develop a low-rent color-group as soon as you can in an attempt to bankrupt your opponents before "heavier" color-groups are developed against you.

10. KNOW WHEN TO CAUSE A BUILDING SHORTAGE.

- If you have only low-rent color-groups, quickly build three or four houses per property, to restrict the availability of houses to owners of high-rent color-groups.
- Never move up to a hotel anywhere if the return of houses to the Bank would enable an opponent to develop an expensive color-group.

Example: the Yellow color-group has just been completed. There are only three houses in the Bank, but six hotels. You own the Light Blues with four houses each. *Do not* buy hotels. Doing so would give the player owning the Yellows an opportunity to build up to hotels on them, if he can afford to. But as things are, no matter his wealth, he can only build one house on each!

11. KNOW HOW TO GET THE MOST OUT OF MORTGAGING.

Mortgaging is essential to raise money at crucial moments in the game. When you need to mortgage, follow this advice:

- Mortgage single properties first. Try not to mortgage a property from a group where you own two or more unless you absolutely have to. (You can't build on a color-group you own if one of its properties is mortgaged.)
- Mortgage single properties to raise cash if it helps you develop a color-group up to at least three houses per property, or hotels on the Light Blues or either Purple group.
- When deciding between two properties, use this priority: try to mortgage the colored property closest to GO, then a single Utility, then any Railroads, then—and only then—a Utility monopoly. (Believe it or not, they produce a lot of cash and you will need cash to unmortgage properties!)

- Exception: Illinois, New York, and Boardwalk have a higher chance of getting landed on than is predicted by this principle, with Illinois the highest. You may want to ignore the above principle and not mortgage these properties in sequence.
- If more expensive color-groups confront you, resist the temptation to mortgage heavily to develop a lower-rent color-group to your limit, unless you're in an "all or nothing" situation late in the game.
- You should pay off mortgages only if you have developed your color-groups to at least three houses per property and can afford to unmortgage.
- When paying off mortgages, pay them off in the reverse order you mortgaged them, *unless* among them is a color-group you can now afford to unmortgage and develop.

12. KNOW HOW TO CONDUCT YOURSELF AS A PLAYER.

This may be the most important principle of all!

- Present yourself as the type of players others won't mind losing to.

Most players abhor losing to:

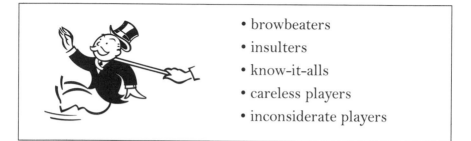

- browbeaters
- insulters
- know-it-alls
- careless players
- inconsiderate players

Most players don't mind losing to opponents who are:

- considerate
- knowledgeable
- diplomatic
- gracious
- savvy

Why is this important? It's because the Monopoly game usually cannot be won without gaining the cooperation of players in trades and financial settlements. If you don't have a reasonable rapport with your opponents, you'll have a tough time making beneficial trades.

If you make enemies, most likely your opponents will gang up on you and shut you out of potential gains in trading. (I've seen it happen a zillion times in tournament play, as I'll tell you about in a later chapter.)

13. KNOW HOW TO TRADE.

Realizing that you'll almost certainly have to make deals is the reason for principle #12 above. And trading is one of the features of the Monopoly game people find most fascinating. It's exciting to pull off a deal that ultimately leads to winning the game.

To make beneficial trades, you need to know the following points:

- Early in the game, trade to get low-cost properties that produce a steady income: namely, the Railroads or Utilities! (Railroads are preferable over Utilities.)
- According to the stage of the game, try to trade for a color-group that can "dominate" quickly (see the Property Tip Sheets).
- To complete such a color-group, your "best" trading materials are: the Railroads, then Utilities, then the Dark Purple monopoly, then single properties that do not yield an opponent a more "dominant" color-group at this time.
- When trading developable properties, try to trade for properties of equal or greater value and that lie closer to Free Parking.
- Use the Property Tip Sheets to determine which color-groups to trade for, based on what you can afford to develop, and which groups have a better chance of paying off.

- If you end up with a complete color-group whose dominance comes later in the game, don't overextend yourself. The lower-rent color-groups are likely to bloody your nose if you deplete your cash too early. Be patient until your cash grows.
- Trade for cash only if your gain is likely to be more than the opponent's potential gain. This means that he or she won't be able to afford to develop a powerful color-group as the result of the trade while you can put the cash to good advantage—by building further or bolstering your cash reserves.
- Use common sense. Make a trade only if you're sure it will improve your chances of winning. Don't allow another player to persuade you to trade just for the sake of trading.
- Remember that when the Monopoly game is played correctly, you cannot include any "caveats" in a trade such as immunity from paying future rents. You can only trade properties you own and cash you have (or can raise through mortgaging or by tearing down buildings).
- When you get an opponent interested in a trade, try to let him do most of the bargaining. You may get more than you thought you could. (Nevertheless, if you feel you can show your opponent why a particular trade is worthwhile for both of you, don't hesitate to demonstrate why.) Try to show your opponent why his demands are too high if you are unwilling to pay his price.

Remember the advice on how to present yourself to your opponents. This is very important while negotiating.

"That's quite a list," I remarked.

"It becomes quite instinctive after you use it for several games," Mr. Monopoly responded. "Naturally, there are other subtleties players will uncover in time. But I've never liked over-burdening anyone with minutiae. You pick up the finer points through play, by applying the main principles. For example, if you know the real value of a property group, you can sense the ramifications of a multiple-property group-forming trade. I could give you dozens of other suggestions, but I won't. I believe everyone who enjoys the Monopoly game will use these principles to his or her best advantage. And since luck plays an

Parker Brothers prints about 50 billion dollars' worth of Monopoly money in one year.

important role in the game, I want players to maintain flexibility, without being locked into too many rigid ideas."

"Did you compile your advice through computer analysis?"

"Mind you now, I've overheated my computer more than once, but my advice is tempered by having watched countless games with real human players. That's why I have so much belief in these principles. They aren't mine so much as they are the winning players' secrets."

"Seems like the best kind to me. What can you tell me about the champion Monopoly players?"

"Ah. That's our next topic!"

Oh, incidentally, remember the game we were playing?

Mr. Monopoly got the Light Blues and the Reds. I got the Light Purples. In rapid order, he developed the Light Blues, drained a good deal of my cash, then clobbered me with three houses on Illinois. Just as the game seemed to be warming up, I was bankrupt.

Oh well, after his "winning tips" sink in, I'll show him a thing or two if he'll entertain a rematch!

MONOPOLY PARTY!

Mr. Monopoly's home sprang to life that evening as eleven guests arrived, via special invitation, to compete in a "mini-tournament." Madge told me she loved gatherings and had created a "winning formula" to make the dinner party a big hit using the Monopoly game as its central theme.

The prior week, she mailed special invitations to each guest, which described the fun that lay ahead. (She was good enough to give me one to reproduce in this book. You can copy it for your own Monopoly party!)

Mr. Monopoly told me how the evening would go.

"Madge is quite a cook, as you know by now. She's created some great food, all inspired by the Monopoly game and Atlantic City. After dinner, our guests will each play two time-limit Monopoly games. Those players with the highest asset totals will take home door prizes. We've set up three tables. At each table four players will compete. You'll be one, of course."

"Of course."

"Now, to get things going quickly, I've devised a technique to get all the Title Deeds and a related amount of cash into circulation the moment the game begins."

Here's how he did it.

Mr. Monopoly had taken four envelopes and sorted the 28 Title Deeds into four "sets." Each set was roughly equal in game value. Then he added some cash to each set—just enough so the actual value of the properties and the cash totaled $2200 per player. As Mr. Monopoly explained, "What I tried to do is set up each game as if it had been going long enough for each player to have completed three circuits around the board *and* collectively to have purchased all the properties. My other objective, to keep things fair, was to assure that the property holdings are about equal in strength."

MR. MONOPOLY MINI-TOURNAMENT PROPERTY/CASH DISTRIBUTIONS

Envelope #1	Envelope #2	Envelope #3	Envelope #4
BALTIC	ORIENTAL	ST. CHARLES	ST. JAMES
MEDIT.	VERMONT	STATES	TENNESSEE
KENTUCKY	CONNECTICUT	VIRGINIA	ATLANTIC
INDIANA	ILLINOIS	NEW YORK	VENTNOR
PACIFIC	BOARDWALK	PARK PLACE	MARVIN GRDS.
N. CAROLINA	PENNA. RR	READING RR	ELECTRIC CO.
PENNA. AVE	B&O RR	SHORT LINE	WATER WORKS
$720 cash	$840 cash	$810 cash	$740 cash

Note: these distributions give each player at least one complete monopoly and encourage immediate trading. Ability to develop a powerful monopoly is roughly equal.

The guests arrived. Four were seated at each table.

After each player took his seat, the dice were rolled. High thrower picked an envelope, opened it, and sorted the properties and cash. In turn, the table's three remaining players did likewise.

The game was now ready to begin.

Aside from a sixty-minute time limit, the rules were identical to the rules in a standard Monopoly game. When time expired, each player totaled his assets and Mr. Monopoly recorded each total on a master score sheet. (See Tournament score sheet on page 145.)

Next, each couple moved to the seats that Mr. Monopoly designated for game #2. Again, the properties and cash were sealed in envelopes and passed out as before. After sixty minutes, the games were stopped and assets totaled. After a break for refreshments, Mr. Monopoly announced the four highest asset totals and awarded the prizes.

"As you can imagine, this concept works great for four, eight, or twelve players," Mr. Monopoly told me afterwards.

I did have a lot of fun—and Madge's treats were great.

MADGE'S MONOPOLY PARTY RECIPES

The Appetizers

Lucky Dice Canapés

Use thick, white bread. Trim crust; cut each slice into four squares. Spread a mixture of ½ cup cream cheese, 2 teaspoons cream, 1 tablespoon anchovy paste, plus a small minced onion, with salt and pepper to taste. Decorate each square with capers arranged to look like sides of a die—from 1 to 6 capers per square.

$1 White Cucumber and Cream Dip

Grate ½ cucumber (peeled and seeded), add 1 cup of sour cream and ¼ teaspoon each of salt and white pepper. Mix thoroughly, then top with additional cucumber gratings.

$5 Pink Shrimp Dip

Blend the following in a food processor: ½ small can of salad shrimp, ¼ cup of sour cream, 2 tablespoons of cream, a few grinds of fresh pepper, 1 small onion, and 1 tablespoon of ketchup. Add the remaining ½ can of shrimp and mix thoroughly. Save a few shrimp for garnish.

$10 Yellow Curry and Carrot Dip

Mix ½ cup mayonnaise, 1 medium grated carrot, and 1½ teaspoons curry powder. Garnish with additional carrot gratings.

$20 Green Avocado Dip

Blend the following in a food processor: ½ cup sour cream, 1 very ripe avocado, 1 minced scallion, and ¼ teaspoon chili powder. Garnish with a well-minced parsley leaf.

$50 Blue Cheese Dip

Combine ½ cup blue cheese dressing, ¼ cup chopped black olives, and ¼ cup sour cream. You may add 2 drops of blue food coloring if desired. Top with ¼ cup crumbled blue cheese.

Charles Darrow may be known as the "father of Monopoly," but Parker Brothers' Robert Barton was perhaps more instrumental in ensuring the game's success. Barton came to terms not only with Knapp Electric, which brought out two "precursor" games, but also with Elizabeth Magie-Phillips, inventor of the Landlord's Game.

The Main Course

Seashore Seafood Salad

Cook 3 cups of dry seashell pasta according to package directions. Chill. Cook 1 pound small salad shrimp for 2½ minutes in boiling water. Chill.

Dressing

⅔ cup olive oil

⅓ cup red wine vinegar

1 tablespoon Dijon mustard

1½ tablespoons Parmesan cheese

1 tablespoon freshly chopped parsley

½ teaspoon Mrs. Dash herb mix

½ teaspoon (10 to 12 grinds) black pepper

¼ teaspoon salt (or to taste)

Mix dressing ingredients in a medium-size bowl with a wire whisk or electric mixer until thick and creamy looking (1-2 minutes). Pour over chilled shrimp and pasta shells. Then add ½ cup cooked broccoli florets, 2 large scallions chopped fine, ½ cup red roasted Italian peppers (available in jars), and ½ cup black olives. Mix all ingredients together and chill until served.

Marinated Monopoly Mignon

Preheat oven to 450 degrees.

Prepare 4-pound tenderloin by trimming fat and any visible tendons. Rub well with olive oil and 1 large minced or pressed garlic clove. Sprinkle generously with black pepper. Refrigerate for at least ½ hour. Do not add salt as this dries out the roast. Cook for 30 minutes for rare, 40 minutes for medium, or 60 minutes for well-done. (Cook in same pan as potatoes, below.)

Park Place Potatoes

Preheat oven to 450 degrees.

Peel 8 large potatoes, rub with olive oil, and sprinkle with onion powder. Line roasting pan with foil, coat with olive oil. Arrange potatoes around edge of pan, allowing room for roast to be added during baking.

Tennessee Avenue Tomatoes

Preheat oven to 450 degrees.

Slice ¼ inch off tops of 8 medium-sized ripe tomatoes. Top with plain bread crumbs, 2 tablespoons per tomato. Sprinkle each with a pinch of basil and small pinch of onion. Top with a small pat of butter. Place in foil-lined pan and add to oven during the final 30 minutes of baking.

Millionaire's Mushroom Sauce

Sauté 1 tablespoon of butter, 1 tablespoon of olive oil, 1 small sliced onion, and 1 cup of sliced mushrooms on medium-high heat in frying pan until brown (4–5 minutes). Mix together 1 cup of water, ½ cup white wine or dry vermouth, 1 teaspoon Worcestershire sauce, 1 tablespoon soy sauce, 1½ teaspoons of corn starch. Add to pan with mushrooms and onions. Cook until hot and bubbling (2–3 minutes). Serve with Monopoly Mignon.

The Dessert

Beauty Contest Banana Yogurt Torte

Preheat oven to 325 degrees.

Put ½ lb. soft butter, 1⅔ cups sugar, and 5 eggs into food processor. Process until smooth. Add 2 ripe bananas and 8 oz. of banana yogurt. Process again until smooth. Add 2 cups cake flour and ¼ teaspoon salt. Process one more time until well-mixed.

Pour into 9-inch springform pan, well-buttered and floured. Bake for 1 hour (or until toothpick in center of cake emerges clean). Top may split. Invert onto cake plate.

Glaze—To one cup of confectioner's sugar, add water, 1 tablespoon at a time (3-4 maximum) until the glaze mixture becomes a thick liquid. Pour over cake, allowing glaze to drip decoratively over the sides. Garnish with sliced bananas brushed with lemon juice to prevent browning.

THE MONOPOLY PARTY INVITATION

An INVITATION
to PLAY a special party version of
the World's Most Popular Board Game:
Monopoly

where: _____

_____

when: _____ *phone:* _____

Following a very special Monopoly dinner,
two 60-minute time-limit games will be played
with splendid prizes awarded to our winners.
A great time is guaranteed! RSVP

VARIATIONS ON THE RULES YOU CAN USE IN STANDARD PLAY

1. Prohibit players who are in Jail from collecting rent, building houses or hotels, or engaging in trading activities.

Ever wonder exactly how much Monopoly money comes with a standard set? The total is $15,140.

2. Make Free Parking a bonus space. At the start of the play place a $500 bill under this corner of the board. All the money due the Bank for fines, taxes, and building repairs goes under Free Parking (but not money from rents, mortgage revenues, or the purchase of Title Deeds or buildings). Whenever a player lands on Free Parking, that player collects the entire sum currently lying there. (The initial $500 is not replaced, once claimed.) Note: this rule makes for long games.

3. Do not allow any player to buy property during his or her first trip around the board. (This variation tends to balance out the disadvantage experienced by those moving last in a game involving five or more players.)

4. Collect $400, rather than $200, for landing on GO. (Continue to collect $200 for passing GO but not landing there.)

5. Allow immunity to be granted as part of a trade. Let's say you trade a property to an opponent who completes a color-group. As part of the trade, that player grants you one or more "free passes" in the event of your landing on the property you traded to him/her.

6. Use "quick auctions" as a way to get all properties into play in a reasonable time. Whenever doubles are thrown, the Banker should auction off the next unowned property clockwise from GO after the player throwing doubles completes his turn.

7. Allow Chance and Community Chest cards to be sold, before they are drawn, by the player who lands on the space. The seller collects the agreed-upon price, then the purchaser draws the card and follows its instructions. Play then proceeds in normal fashion—with the player to the seller's left rolling next.

"CLOCKWATCHER" GAME VARIATIONS— FOR THOSE IN A HURRY!

Time Limit Monopoly Game

Before starting play, simply agree on an ending time. Ninety minutes is a good suggestion (preliminary rounds during official tournaments cease after ninety minutes). At the expiration of time, the Banker halts play (after the turn in progress is completed) and each player totals the value of his or her assets.

Short Monopoly Game

The Banker shuffles all the Title Deeds and deals two to each player (the remainder stay in the Bank). Each player pays for the deeds he or she receives. Permit players to build hotels after three houses are erected on each lot of a color-group. (Eliminate the four house level entirely.) If hotels are broken down, they are worth four houses each (rather than five). The game ends after the second player has gone bankrupt. The remaining players total their assets. Highest assets wins!

MONOPOLY FOR KEEPS

"Monopoly can be played on two levels," Mr. Monopoly reminded me. "It's for those who enjoy the social interaction it provides, and for those who love to compete. Now, for someone who loves to compete *and* become the best player he or she can be, there is the highly charged world of Monopoly tournaments.

"A new United States Champion is crowned every three years; the following year a new World Champion emerges from a field of twenty or more national champs, including the U.S. champ. The World Tournaments have been held in cities like Monte Carlo and Palm Beach, not to mention right here in Atlantic City."

"That sounds exciting. How does one enter such a tournament?"

Mr. Monopoly proceeded to give me the details of how most tournaments have been organized.

1. Local Tournaments

Soon after each World Championship is completed, Hasbro officials begin to assist organizations around the country in holding local Monopoly tournaments that will go toward crowning the next United States champion.

Groups like the Boy and Girl Scouts, the Department of Public Works, and the Chamber of Commerce will sponsor these tournaments. Notices appear in local newspapers to invite everyone interested.

On the day of the tournament, players gather and are read a list of procedures and rule clarifications. (This list is printed in this chapter.) Players are instructed to follow the same procedural rules that are enforced in both the U.S. and World Championship tournaments.

Players play three 90-minute time-limit games. At the conclusion of each game, the tournament officials tally the asset value accumulated by each player. At the end of all three rounds, the player with the highest asset total is the local champion— and possibly the state's champ as well.

2. The State Champion

When all the local tournaments are completed, the asset totals of all the local champs are compared. Hasbro officials crown the local champ with the highest asset value the state's champion.

How Assets Are Determined

Since the tournament games are governed by a time limit, many players will still be "in the game" when time expires. They have their assets tallied. (For those who go bankrupt, their asset total is 0, of course.)

Assets consist of:

• cash on hand

• full value of unmortgaged properties owned

• mortgaged value of any property owned which is mortgaged

• full stated value of all houses and hotels owned

Note: GET OUT OF JAIL FREE cards have no value.

The sample tournament score sheet on page 145 is like the score sheets used at tournament levels; you can use this for your own games.

Finance and Fortune, two "precursor" games, were eventually published by Parker Brothers—though both were substantially modified to clearly separate them from Mr. Monopoly's game. Fortune did not succeed, but Finance was published well into the 1970s.

MONOPOLY® TOURNAMENT SCORE SHEET

Property	No Buildings		With Buildings					
	Mort-gaged	Fully Owned	With 1 House	With 2 Houses	With 3 Houses	With 4 Houses	With a Hotel	
Mediterranean Avenue	$30	$60	$110	$160	$210	$260	$310	$
Baltic Avenue	30	60	110	160	210	260	310	$
Oriental Avenue	50	100	150	200	250	300	350	$
Vermont Avenue	50	100	150	200	250	300	350	$
Connecticut Avenue	60	120	170	220	270	320	370	$
St. Charles Place	70	140	240	340	440	540	640	$
States Avenue	70	140	240	340	440	540	640	$
Virginia Avenue	80	160	260	360	460	560	660	$
St. James Place	90	180	280	380	480	580	680	$
Tennessee Avenue	90	180	280	380	480	580	680	$
New York Avenue	100	200	300	400	500	600	700	$
Kentucky Avenue	110	220	370	520	670	820	970	$
Indiana Avenue	110	220	370	520	670	820	970	$
Illinois Avenue	120	240	390	540	690	840	990	$
Atlantic Avenue	130	260	410	560	710	860	1010	$
Ventnor Avenue	130	260	410	560	710	860	1010	$
Marvin Gardens	140	280	430	580	730	880	1030	$
Pacific Avenue	150	300	500	700	900	1100	1300	$
North Carolina Avenue	150	300	500	700	900	1100	1300	$
Pennsylvania Avenue	160	320	520	720	920	1120	1320	$
Park Place	175	350	550	750	950	1150	1350	$
Boardwalk	200	400	600	800	1000	1200	1400	$
Reading Railroad	100	200						$
Pennsylvania Railroad	100	200						$
B&O Railroad	100	200						$
Short Line	100	200						$
Electric Company	75	150						$
Water Works	75	150						$

A
$

Total Property

	$1 Bills	$5 Bills	$10 Bills	$20 Bills	$50 Bills	$100 Bills	$500 Bills
Number Held							
Cash Value	$	$	$	$	$	$	$

→

B
$

Total Cash

A+B
$

Grand Total

Name

Address

City

State   Zip

Telephone

Name of Organization

Place of Tournament

Date

Signature of Player

Signature of Banker/Referee

Signature of Notary Public

Sample tournament score sheet you can use for your own games.

3. The United States Championship

Approximately a year after the first local tournament is held, the process is completed and all state champions are determined. Champions are declared in all fifty states, plus Washington, D.C., and Puerto Rico. Each is now invited, with all expenses paid by Parker Brothers, to attend the United States Championship. This prestigious event has been held in cities like New York, Washington, Atlantic City, and Los Angeles. Hordes of reporters and TV cameramen converge to cover the multiday event.

Prior to the start of play, the tournament's Chief Judge briefs the official Bankers. These men and women are usually real-life bankers from banks in the city where the tournament is being held.

Then, the Chief Judge briefs all the contestants, and answers all questions about procedures and rules interpretations. He reviews the same Tournament Guidelines that each player first encountered in his or her local tournament.

MONOPOLY®

Parker Brothers Real Estate Trading Game

TOURNAMENT POINTS TO REMEMBER

1. To raise money to pay *debts,* only houses and hotels can be sold back to the bank (at half price), never properties. If a debt is owed to another player, properties may be sold to a third player only if sufficient money is raised to cover the debt. If not, the properties are turned over *as is* (and not mortgaged if unmortgaged at the time the debt is incurred.)

2. The owner may not collect his *rents* if he fails to ask for it before the second player following throws the dice. This means: Player A lands on your property. Player B has his turn. You must collect your rent before Player C throws the dice.

3. If you throw a doubles to get out of Jail, you move forward that number of spaces as your turn. You do not throw again. However, if you pay to get out of Jail prior to rolling, and you throw doubles, you may throw again as usual.

4. Though you need not disclose how much *money* you have, you must keep your money on the table in plain view at all times.

5. All trades are based on assets owned at the time of the trade. No options or immunity from paying future rents may be granted, nor may partnerships be formed.

6. Trading is permitted during a player's turn or in between other players' turns, but not during an opposing player's turn.

7. Players cannot sell *Chance* or *Community Chest* cards prior to revealing them to other players.

8. Players may *not* consult or seek advice from friends or game observers while the game is in progress.

9. *Tokens* used in Tournament play *must* be from the game itself.

10. While a *Building Shortage* exists, players desiring to buy the houses remaining in the bank have priority over those wishing to break down hotels.

11. In *Preliminary Games,* when only *two* players remain, no further trades or deals are permitted.

As in the local tournaments, a series of three 90-minute preliminary games are played. A Chief Banker also serves as official timekeeper. He or she also dispenses specially coded money to visually assure that money in play is valid. Assets are tallied after each game and verified by the Chief Banker and his committee. When all three games are finished, the four players with the highest asset totals are announced as the finalists.

The four finalists and the reigning United States Champion now compete in a final five-player, winner-takes-all game *without* any time limit.

When the excitement-packed final game is over, a new United States Champion emerges victorious!

This player is now invited to attend the World Championship, held the following year.

4. The World Monopoly Championship

National champions from thirty-plus nations send their winners to attend the World Tournament. (Players in other countries compete in a similar manner to the United States to determine their national champion, as supervised by official Monopoly game licensees (or subsidiaries of Hasbro) in those nations.

The World Tournament is often held in a glamorous city on a distant continent, but sometimes it is held in the United States because many national champions wish to come to the birthplace of the Monopoly game.

At the start of the tournament, the Chief Judge briefs the Bankers and the contestants, as at the U.S. Championship. Again, three 90-minute preliminary games are played. Assets are tallied and the four players with the highest totals will compete, along with the current world champ, in the final game.

Played without a time limit, the final game is both an intense game and a media experience. Reporters crowd against the perimeter of the playing area (which is usually a large round table on a raised platform) and on the risers provided so they can see the proceedings. Seated at the table are the five finalists, the Chief Judge, and Chief Banker. Slightly behind some of the players are official interpreters to aid those players who do not easily understand and speak English.

Television lights illuminate the scene, cameras quietly whir, and the game begins. In championship game play, players first roll to see which player has first choice of playing token. Then, each rolls one more time to determine sequence of play. Only then do they take seats—the player with the highest throw, who will play first, sits to the Chief Judge's left, followed on his left by the player with the second-highest throw, etc.

During play, the Chief Banker handles all transactions with the Bank, while the Chief Judge answers all questions and resolves any dispute promptly. Usually, he is also equipped with a microphone so the crowd can hear the progress of the game as they watch it on large television monitors.

The game soon builds in intensity. These are the best players in the world and the quality of the game usually reflects this fact. Key trades are made; monopolies are formed. Buildings rise.

Surprisingly soon, one player goes bankrupt, then another, then another.

Finally, the last two players lock heads in a survival of the fittest. The press converges closer still. The crowd reacts in unison whenever one of these two "combatants" is granted a stay in Jail, and the opponent's color-groups are temporarily avoided. Groans—or cheers—are heard whenever a big rent is due. Each player stretches his resources to the limit. It is "now or never" time, and the maximum number of buildings are on the board.

Suddenly, one player breathes a sigh of relief as the crowd oohs and aahs. The opposing player has landed on a powerhouse color-group and can't meet the rent. He or she tears down hotels and houses, mortgages property, and watches victory start to slip away.

The dice tumble for the last few times. The player on the ropes lands once more on a powerful color-group. This time it is over. Handshakes are exchanged as the Chief Judge hurries to place the champion's sash over the winner's shoulder before the press closes in.

Minutes later, at the main podium, the finalists are honored and given their prizes (usually a check). Then the winner is presented and handed the Monopoly plaque commemorating his or her great win, and awarded whatever grand prize awaits. (Grand prizes from past championships have included a Monopoly game filled with *real* cash, a $10,000 shopping spree, and a fabulous vacation.)

Television cameras now surround the Champion as he is interviewed in rapid fire fashion. By the next morning, he or she is seen all over America on programs like *Today* and *Good Morning America.* Later that evening, the event is again recounted on the network evening news. And since many of the world champions have come from other countries, the news spreads internationally just as quickly.

"Impressive, isn't it?" Mr. Monopoly concluded.

"It seems only fitting that the world's most popular game should crown its world champion after such a thorough series of contests."

"Yes, and as a result, the champions know they've earned their titles."

"What are these champions like?" I asked. "Have past winners been bankers, people involved with money? Or bright youngsters and students who know the game inside out?"

"Actually, the past champions have been from many walks of life and of many different ages. But I'm disappointed to say that there has yet to be a female declared World Champion." Mr. Monopoly now handed me another sheet of paper. "Here's a list of the United States and World Champions since the first official tournament was held in 1973."

I accepted the list and quickly reviewed its contents.

"You may notice that tournaments were held annually from 1973 through 1975, then periodically since. That's because, at first, the tournament was pretty much a United States affair with one European representative competing against three or four regional United States champs. But beginning in 1978, a true world tournament was held. As I explained, to set the stage for a world tournament, two years of lower-level play is required to correctly identify the national champions. So time is needed in between.

"I've attended all of these great events," Mr. Monopoly announced with pride in his voice. "I know these players and—as I told you earlier—have compiled my winning advice based on their tactics and strategies."

"Tell me about some of the most exciting moments in the tournaments."

"Ah, of course. There have been quite a few. Each bears its own lessons."

HIGHLIGHTS FROM TOURNAMENT PLAY

Monopoly tournaments are lively affairs. Perhaps this is due to the fact that people of all ages and walks of life have won the privilege of competing. Their diversity and level of excitement certainly brighten a Monopoly tournament until it clearly outshines the staid, head-to-head atmosphere of, say, a chess championship. Perhaps it is due to the role that luck plays in each game, turning seemingly predictable outcomes into roller coaster rides of uncertainty.

Perhaps it is simply because the Monopoly game is such an ingenious creation that no two games are ever alike.

Perhaps it is because so many millions of people know and love the game.

Perhaps all of these things are what enliven the tournaments.

1975

In the early tournaments, the process of crowning a Monopoly champion underwent a gradual evolution as the kinks were worked out. After the 1973, '74, and '75 tournaments, it became clear that the procedures clearly favored a U.S. player to win the World Championship. There was no single U.S. national champ back then, just three or four regional champions, all of whom would compete against a European champion in the finals.

In 1975, it was decided to add some luster to the European Championship by holding it in Reykjavik, Iceland—the scene of Bobby Fisher's now-legendary chess championship.

The tournament occurred in mid-November. Iceland is a cold, misty country to begin with, but during the tournament it rained almost all the time. As a result, the press isolated on the remote island had little to do in between the preliminary games except drink. They became quite a rowdy bunch.

The eventual champion, John Mair of Ireland, was one in kind with the press. He drank as much as the best of them. In fact, he later boasted that the match turned in his favor when he inadvertently dropped the dice into his glass of beer instead of the dice cup provided for this tournament. Why was this mistake to his advantage? "I moved on to gin and tonic," he explained.

Mair not only won in Iceland, but just two days later in Washington, D.C., he beat all of his American opponents to become the first non-American World Champion.

Each year, the makers of Monopoly produce more than twice as much play money as the U.S. Mint does actual money!

While young Mair did not necessarily help the "family-friendly" image of the game, his foreign residence established the Monopoly game as a valid forum for international competition.

Parker Brothers took the results of this and the prior two tournaments to heart and decided 1) not to hold tournaments on an annual basis, but rather to allow more time for competition to be narrowed down from the local to the world level, and 2) to improve the equality of the world championship by having the national winner from each country present. No longer would there be a European Champion and several U.S. players in the finals.

1977

Twenty contestants gathered in Monte Carlo in October of 1977 to play the first true international championship. Nineteen countries were represented, plus the reigning champion from Ireland.

John Mair brought his lucky straw hat with him, a jovial light-hearted personality, and his usual thirst for beer. The Irishman won his first game of the four that were to be played. He played the remaining three games well enough to make it into the finals.

The climatic game featured players from Britain, Germany, Italy, and Singapore to compete with Mair.

The game was marked, from the start, by a cautious attitude among all players. Trading was nonexistent for fear of giving any edge to an opponent. Then, after a thirty-three-minute negotiation, requiring the translation services of multiple interpreters, the first trade was announced. Singapore acquired the yellows, Britain claimed the greens, Germany acquired the coveted oranges, and Mair took the Boardwalk monopoly. Italy was left out in the cold (a situation that was nearly repeated three years later).

Italy was unable to swing a deal for the Reds; he went bankrupt quickly to Singapore. The Greens, notorious for their bad luck in tournament play, failed Britain, and Singapore claimed another bankruptcy victim. To the surprise of many, Germany could not turn the magical Oranges to his advantage. He too fell. Mair surveyed the carnage and realized the odds against him were too great. Graciously, he conceded.

Quiet, thoughtful Cheng Seng Kwa of Singapore—a sales executive—had dramatically claimed the world title.

The lessons to be learned from this tournament are quite basic:

1. When the rush to trade for color-groups becomes a stampede, do not get trampled and left out. You must emerge with the best complete color-group you can to avoid inevitable bankruptcy.

2. The best color-group to obtain in a trade is one on a side of the board adjacent to Free Parking, preferably the most expensive you can afford to develop to the three-house level. (Kwa took the Yellows and did just that.)

1980

The 1980 championship was one of the best ever. And it was preceded the prior fall by probably the most thrilling United States Championship ever played.

Let's start with that game.

The reigning U.S. Champion was Dana Terman, a 24-year-old Maryland native and salesman for an auto dealership. Terman developed a reputation as a tough and wily player who knew the game inside and out. In the finals, his most formidable competitor—and the crowd and media's favorite—was an unflappable 10-year-old named Angelo Repole from Staten Island. Repole had already beaten four competitors in their thirties in the Eastern Regional Finals. (This was the last year the state champs were grouped at regional tournaments to determine the U.S. finalists.) By the time the U.S. Championship rolled around, the press was calling him the "Monopoly Whiz Kid."

One of Terman's advantages was having had the privilege to attend each of the four regional championships. As a result, he had the line on his opponents; he knew Repole was the most resolute of the bunch, the one with the necessary killer instinct to wipe out any opponent on the ropes. Repole had never seen Terman in action but heard of his remarkable comebacks in the Monte Carlo tournament. While Terman could not overcome some bad luck in Monte Carlo, he did remarkably well and just missed the finals. Unquestionably, Terman played intently and probably knew the Monopoly game better than the prior U.S. champs.

Repole was remarkable for many reasons. Yes, he was cute and outspoken, but he was also a marvelous player who had only six months of playing experience prior to the tournament! He had grown up street-smart, in a broken home. He stood up to players twice his age and was not intimidated in the crucial deal-making aspect of the game. In fact, through hard-line tactics, he usually took charge in trading sessions!

In his regional victory, good luck also helped Angelo. He landed on all three Light Purple properties in successive trips around the board. He completed the color-group and exploited it quickly and decisively.

Now, in the U.S. Championship, played in the center of the Palace Restaurant (the country's most expensive until it went bankrupt), Angelo found his luck mirroring his earlier experience. He got the complete Light Purple color-group early.

Predictably, the other three players—whose fangs lacked the venom of Angelo and Dana—quietly went bankrupt

The press huddled closer, sensing the final kill. While Dana had used all of his savvy to stay in the game, he now found himself with a lot of properties but little cash. His only hope lay with the Dark Blue color-group and the red hotel standing so dramatically on Boardwalk and the four houses crowding Park Place. Angelo rolled. Once more he skipped past Boardwalk, landing on GO. Dana was not as lucky. States Avenue and its hotel greeted him with a $750 rent. Angelo cheered reflexively. Most of Dana's undeveloped properties were flipped white-side-up. Only mortgage money kept him alive.

Then Angelo's luck seemed complete. He landed in Jail. The bubble gum in his mouth popped faster now; he looked forward to a long stay while Dana remained exposed, dancing towards the minefields located on St. Charles, States, and Virginia Avenues.

Then, on his very first turn in Jail, Angelo threw double-sixes. (The odds of throwing two 6's are 1 in 36, or about 3%.) Twelve spaces later Angelo touched down on the red question mark separating Kentucky from Indiana Avenue.

Even before Angelo drew the card, Terman knew he had won. Observant spectators also knew why a slight grin was already forming on Terman's lips, beneath his moustache.

Previously, fifteen Chance cards had been drawn. Only one of the sixteen remained unseen. (The odds of any one card being the sixteenth drawn are 1 out of 16, or about 6% probability.)

Angelo flipped over the card.

It read: ADVANCE TOKEN TO BOARDWALK.

The combined odds of 576 to 1 claimed its victim.

Angelo landed on Boardwalk and owed $2000 in rent. He had the money to pay the bill, but now Terman unmortgaged the Yellows and built houses on them as well as the reds. Angelo was quickly outgunned.

The Light Purple color-group was soon razed. In short order, Dana Terman accepted the 10-year-old's brave handshake and breathed a sigh of deep relief.

The following spring, on the lovely island of Bermuda, Terman arrived to compete in the World Championship. Competing against him were twenty-one international champions, including Cheng Seng Kwa of Singapore. Among the others was a young microwave engineer from Italy, who spoke reasonable English and maintained an easy style that endeared him to the press. (Fortunately, it didn't rain much on this island and the press consumed only a fraction of the spirits imbibed on Iceland five years earlier.)

The preliminary rounds were not very suspenseful. Notably, Kwa was wiped out in every game. Later, he admitted to not practicing since Monte Carlo. Terman made the finals effortlessly. The Italian, Cesare Bernabei, squeaked in, finishing fourth among the five players who qualified for the final game.

Things did not go well for Bernabei at first. He found himself with Atlantic Avenue, two Light Purples, a railroad, and a utility at a point in the game when Terman was attempting to get the upper hand via the expensive Greens. But a not-so-strange thing happened. The other three players, sensing Terman would win, stopped dealing with him. Bernabei found himself the beneficiary of this change in attitude: the French player dealt him the third Light Purple, turning down a better deal from Dana. Terman's reputation as a hard-driving, somewhat uncaring player was well established by the final round. The spectators sensed the "stop Dana at any cost" attitude, but Bernabei did not openly relish the value of this backlash. Without fanfare, but with obvious grace, Bernabei accepted the hand of each player he bankrupted in turn.

Now Terman was in deep trouble.

Again, as in New York, the Light Purple color-group lay in wait for him. Dana's token sat on GO when he rolled the dice. He threw an eleven and didn't even bother to pick up his token. Cash-poor and heavily mortgaged, Dana knew the hotel on St. Charles spelled defeat. Many players still seated around the table stood up after Dana rose and shook Bernabei's hand.

In so doing, someone jostled the table inadvertently. No one seemed to notice until a few moments later when the awards ceremony was about to begin. Suddenly, one of the other defeated finalists looked down at the board and yelled out, "Wait! It's not over."

Looking back, the crowd of people saw that Dana's token was sitting askew on Mediterranean Avenue. The Electric Company lay eleven spaces from Mediterranean, not St. Charles Place.

The Chief Judge was asked to rule. He declared that the decision stood, the game was over. (Later he explained that not only was he certain that Terman's token had started on GO, but Dana's silent reaction to the other finalist's claim was proof that the token had been misplaced.)

Then a television cameraman spoke up. "I have it on video-tape if you want to check what happened."

The Chief Judge huddled with Parker Brothers officials who said they'd back his decision if he wanted it to stand. "No," he replied. "Let's look at the tape, so there won't possibly be a question of doubt."

The tape verified the facts. After Terman stood up, the token had bounced forward one space.

The charming Italian was, indeed, the new World Champion. Several lessons emerge from these two exciting games:

1. In the Monopoly game, it is not over until it is over. (I'm sure Yogi Berra would agree.)

2. Knowing the identity of Chance and Community Chest cards drawn can provide an insight into what will happen near the bottom of each deck. That can influence your tactical decisions.

3. Age is not a barrier to success at the Monopoly game. Few other games can boast of this advantage.

4. The Green properties do not seem to produce winners in tournament play while the Light Purples seem to decide more than their share of victors.

5. If you are not the type of player your peers don't mind losing to, you'll have a tougher time winning than otherwise.

1983

In the prior year, the United States Championship heralded the arrival of a true fifty-state competition. In Washington, D.C., all the state champs competed in the same room for the first time. There, in the halls of the Corcoran Gallery, the new champion was determined. He was Jerry Dausman, a 29-year-old accountant from the tournament's hometown. Among the players he defeated was Dana Terman. Dausman presented himself as a pleasant, intelligent player. Clearly not as intent as Terman, he managed to win just the same.

One of the more controversial moments in the tournament occurred in the second preliminary round when one player decided to reduce his three hotels to twelve houses to block an opponent from buying the houses in the Bank. From this incident forward, this tactic was outlawed in tournament play. The Chief Judge ruled that forcing a building shortage is only valid by freezing property development at the four-house level. By moving up to hotels, a player forgoes his right to create a housing shortage if other players wish to purchase the houses remaining in the Bank.

In 1983, the World Championship took place by the sea in Palm Beach, Florida, at the venerable Breakers Hotel.

This tournament was well-played but largely uneventful. Cesare Bernabei did not fare well, admitting he had limited his practicing to a few games with his 10-year-old niece.

This tournament featured another youngster—14-year-old Jason Mallet of the United Kingdom, who willingly offered his winning advice to the press, and whose skill catapulted him into the final round. There he faced four older players including the champs from Peru, Venezuela, Austria, and Australia (who climbed from 9th place to 4th in the final round to squeak into the final game).

Mallet did well early on, landing on all three Light Purples. But after two of his opponents went bankrupt, he was confronted by a formidable array of houses on Boardwalk and Park Place, which soon made him the latest victim of methodical Greg Jacobs of Australia. Jacobs was a likable man who had avoided trouble with artful reasoning to keep his opponents from making damaging deals. Soon, the final opponent, Peru, bowed to the Aussie's four-color-group stranglehold on the board. (1983 was a banner year for Australia, in many arenas, including the Monopoly game!)

Jacobs's victory, smooth and well-played, was largely due to his instinctive knowledge of the value of each color-group. He had been playing the Monopoly game since he was five! While his nearly flawless play prevented any major surprises in the final game, what happened afterwards was memorable.

The following day, he was entitled to spend his winnings—$10,000—in a four-hour shopping spree on prestigious Worth Avenue.

What would he buy? the press wondered. Imported Italian shoes? Gold jewelry? Diamonds?

Jacobs calmly purchased a scarf for his wife, a few toys for his kids. Then he walked into a broker's office and plunked the remainder of the money— $9700—into precious metals and stocks.

A 31-year-old real estate agent, Jacobs appreciated the value of investing in real life as much as in the Monopoly game. Taking his precepts to heart, he played for the future.

(Incidentally, the stock he purchased tripled in the next three years.)

Lessons learned from this tournament include:

1. As always, you have to be diplomatic and win the respect of your opponents.
2. If you let a good opponent off the ropes, you'll regret it.
3. Knowing the true value and importance of each color-group will surely improve your chances of winning.

1985

In November 1984, the United States Championship took place in Union Station, Los Angeles. There, Jim Forbes, a jovial bald-headed accountant from Florida unseated Jerry Dausman to claim the title. The following September, Forbes arrived in Atlantic City to do battle with twenty foreign champions.

In a ballroom of the Claridge Casino, overlooking Park Place and the Boardwalk, the final game took place on a drizzly afternoon following a long bus ride from New York (where the preliminary games had been played).

Twenty-five-year-old Jason Bunn of England took the contest. Bunn was a test engineer from Leeds, England, who practiced every lunch hour with his work mates—an intelligent and analytical bunch to say the least! Luck was with him as—like Angelo Repole and James Mallet before him—he completed a color-group on the Light Purples without having to make a trade. He gained a quick advantage over all four of his opponents (Peru, Japan, Austria, and Jacobs of Australia) and won handily. His last remaining opponent was Greg Jacobs, whose initial luck was nonexistent, as he did not acquire many good properties early in the game. Again, it was his skill and knowledge that overcame that handicap and kept his hope alive for so long.

Bunn stood ready to defend his crown in London in the fall of 1988.

The lessons from this tournament are largely a repeat of prior lessons, but also:

1. Practice and actual playing experience are invaluable.
2. The more situations you face and deal with prior to a tournament, the better your chances of knowing the right way out of a jam, or the right way to maximize an advantage to turn uncertainty into victory.

1987

The United States Championship of 1987 featured the most evenly matched group of finalists ever. Once again the tournament was held in Washington, D.C.

The four finalists competing against Jim Forbes included the winners of the state championships in Indiana, Colorado, New Jersey, and Florida.

In prior tournaments, the lack of a time limit on the final round did not impede the progress of the game. Virtually all such games were over within two hours.

For a long time in this final, history seemed to be no guide. So evenly matched were these five players, and so impartial was Lady Luck, that almost 1½ hours of playing time elapsed before serious trading discussions got going. Strangely, the deadlock was broken when Paul Ingray of New Jersey accepted the Light Blues as his complete color-group in the chain reaction of trades that occurred. Ingray had been a player to be feared in the preliminary rounds. Some of his opponents regarded him as outright ruthless and overly intent. Yet, in a most gracious gesture, he conceded to this potentially unfavorable deal. Shortly after Jim Forbes went bankrupt (unable to fully develop his Reds), Ingray followed.

The reason the Light Blues were a bad deal for Ingray is that their rentals, even with hotels, could not match the potential income of the other color-groups that developed in front of him

on the board. Yet by making that deal, Ingray allowed the game
to conclude within the next forty minutes.

The game otherwise proceeded in flawless fashion. There
were no disputes; each player seemed to make the best decision
every time. But time took its toll and Gary Peters, armed with
the Oranges and Reds, won a clear victory over Noah Burcyzk of
Indiana and Mark Rice of Colorado.

The lesson from this tournament is an important one:
*When a massive trading session occurs, don't agree to accept a
low-priced color-group, even if substantial cash comes with it.
If a lot of cash has entered the game, development of the expensive
color-groups is a sure thing. Your position, with a low-end color-
group, will erode almost immediately. Resist the pressure to
"make something happen" and hold out for a better deal.*

Equally exciting tournaments and champions emerged
during the 1992, 1995, 2000, and 2004 World Championships.
Here is a list of all the winners.

THE HONOR ROLL OF MONOPOLY CHAMPIONS

Year	Location	U.S. Representative	World Champion
1973	Washington, DC	**Lee Bayrd** TV writer	**Lee Bayrd** U.S.
1974	Washington, DC	**Alvin Aldridge** student	**Alvin Aldridge** U.S.
1975	Washington, DC	**Gus Gostomelsky** accountant	**John Mair** UK
1977	Monte Carlo	**Dana Terman** bus. mgr.	**Cheng Seng Kwa** Singapore
1980	Bermuda	**Dana Terman** bus. mgr.	**Cesare Bernabei** Italy
1983	Palm Beach, FL	**Jerome Dausman** accountant	**Greg Jacobs** New Zealand
1985	Atlantic City, NJ	**Jim Forbes** accountant	**Jason Bunn** UK
1988	London, England	**Gary Peters** banker	**Ikuo Hyakuta** Japan
1992	Berlin, Germany	**Gary Peters** banker	**Joost von Oren** Netherlands
1995	Monte Carlo	**Roger Craig** saleman	**Christopher Woo** Hong Kong
2000	Toronto, Canada	**Matt Gissel** student	**Yutaka Okada** Japan
2004	Tokyo, Japan	**Matt McNally** student	**Antonio Fernandez** Spain

LOCAL TOURNAMENTS

Here in their own words, is the advice and opinions several Monopoly champions have offered during and after their participation in these tournaments.

Angelo Repole—1979 Eastern Regional Champ; 2nd place finish in U.S. Championship. Age: 10.

Q. What is your strategy?
A. "Buy every property you land on, except don't overextend yourself. Don't overextend when building, and hope that luck doesn't overcome your strategies."

Q. Do you get nervous when playing players older than yourself?
A. "No!"

Dana Terman—1977 and 1979 U.S. Monopoly Champ. Age: 23.

Q. What is your advice for winning the game?
A. "Know the rules inside and out, and use them for maximum advantage. Always play to drive another player out of the game as quickly as possible."

Cesare Bernabei—Italian.
1980 World Champion. Age: 26.

Q. How do you win?

A. "I keep trying to get the best deal I can without giving away too much. Once you make a bad trade you can't recover. I try to show the other guy why the trade proposed is good for him too."

Jerome Dausman—1982
U.S. Champion. Age: 29.

Q. What advice do you have for Monopoly players out there?

A. "Play with good sportsmanship but also play smart. Know the rules and basic strategies and use them well."

James Mallet—1983 United Kingdom Champion
and World Champion at age 14.

Q. Does it bother you to play older players?

A. "It doesn't bother me to play older, more-experienced players."

Q. What is your advice for winning?

A. "Play the best game you can and hope the dice go your way. I wouldn't tell you all my strategies, but I will tell you I like to play a 'housing shortage' [strategy] instead of building up to hotels . . . because it prevents your opponents from building fully."

Q. What has the Monopoly game taught you?

A. "I started playing when I was four. I learned to count on it, learned to read on it, and learned to lose on it, so it's helped me to grow up!"

Greg Jacobs—Australia. 1983 World Champion. Age: 31.

Q. What about hotels?

A. "Don't buy hotels. If possible, buy only houses. Tie them up and create a housing shortage."

Q. Is the Monopoly game luck or skill?

A. "It's a factor of both luck and skill. If you're skillful, you can minimize the impact of bad luck."

Q. Any other tips for winning?

A. "Always buy everything and build your way up as the game goes on."

Q. When you play, do you feel you're playing for real?

A. "No, I don't have any vision that I'm playing for real properties and the like. It's just a great game that I'm playing."

Q. Do you feel bad bankrupting an opponent?

A. "Not at all."

Jim Forbes—1984 U.S. Champion. Age: 34.

Q. What's your secret strategy?
A. "Buy everything [unowned] you land on."

Q. Do you feel bad when you bankrupt an opponent?
A. "Not in the least!"

Tommy Glynn—1985 Irish Champion (did not make 1985 final round in World Championship). Age: 20.

Q. What do you find appealing about the Monopoly game?
A. "It has a strong human element when you're wheeling and dealing. It's like life itself."

If one or both dice roll off the board, or land or lean against a card deck, the roll is invalid. Roll them again.

Jason Bunn—1985 United Kingdom and World Champion. Age: 25.

Q. Is the Monopoly game skill or luck?

A. "Fifty-fifty skill and luck. I equate [the Monopoly game] with a game of poker. You get cards as you go around the board. And what cards you get you've got to play [to your advantage] like in a game of poker."

Q. In other words, it's the luck of the draw and then your skill determines how well you do with [the Title Deeds]?

A. "That's right."

Gary Peters—1987 U.S. Champion. Age: 42.

Q. Who did you compete against in the U.S. Championship?

A. "I competed against all the state champions who ranged in age from 14 to 54."

Q. How tough was the final game?

A. "It was the toughest game I've played and this was the most wholesome event I have ever participated in."

Roger Craig—1995 U.S. Champion. Age: 36.

Q. When you returned home after you won the U.S. Championship, what happened?

A. "I got quite a welcome in Harrisburg, Illinois. The mayor recognized my achievement, as did the local Chamber of commerce. They gave me a plaque and designated an entire week as 'Roger Craig Week.' "

Christopher Woo—1995 World Champion. Age: 37.

Q. How do you interrelate with your opponents when playing the Monopoly game?

A. "I like to quickly get acquainted with my opponents and build relationships with them. I find that helps when the trading starts."

Q. Is skill important in winning?

A. "Very much so. But I also held on to my 'lucky marble' during the World Championship."

Matthew McNally—2003 U.S. Champion. Age: 22

Q. What's your best tip, Matt?

A. Put, aside all preconceived notions and get to know your opponents' true strengths and weaknesses. Exploit them, but also play respectfully.

"And there you have it," Mr. Monopoly summarized. "The succinct advice of the real experts. Use it well."

Mr. Monopoly invited me into his private den. "Welcome to my inner sanctum," he joked as he led me inside.

To my amazement, the den was papered with Monopoly gameboard labels. At closer glance I realized the game board labels were in many different languages, each sporting different street names.

"They're all here," Mr. Monopoly exclaimed. "All eighty versions in twenty-six different languages."

I took notes, smiling at the change of names of Boardwalk from country to country.

Boardwalk: U.S.

Mayfair: U.K.

Rue de la Paix: France

Schlossalle: Germany

Paseo de Gracia: Spain

Efoff Street: South Africa

Kalverstrat: The Netherlands

"My Monopoly game is played around the world," Mr. Monopoly said with delight. "Over five hundred million players have enjoyed it since 1935. And that's why every World Championship is such a big event worldwide."

THE GAME'S MANY VERSIONS

As he was talking, I couldn't help notice the impressive collection of Monopoly games on display in a lighted glass case.

I saw the latest Standard Edition (including the new Speed Die for faster play). This is the most popular of the world's most famous game's many versions. And then I noticed the current Deluxe Edition with its fine components and added accessories. Nearby were the new Mega and Here & Now Editions. They make you feel richer than ever imagined. The first has more properties, a bigger board, skyscrapers, bus tickets, and the nifty new Speed Die for pleasurably fast play. The latter features million-dollar bills, all-new property names, and modern tokens.

I smiled anew when I saw the Monopoly Jr. game. "It's specially designed for kids a bit too young for the regular Monopoly game. Playing Monopoly Jr. prepares them for the 'big time,'" added Mr. Monopoly. "And look, my nephews are pictured on the cover. They helped with the playtesting too!" Mr. Monopoly explained that the properties pictured on its colorful board were amusements on the Boardwalk. Players purchase ticket booths and collect fees when their opponents land on them. Adding, subtracting, and multiplying are all part of the fun.

The Monopoly Game, with new Speed Die for faster play

© 2007 Hasbro

Reproduction of the game's 1935 Deluxe Edition
© 1935, 2002 Hasbro

Monopoly: The Card Game

All the highlights
of the board game
with faster play.

created by Winning Moves, Inc.
© 2000 Hasbro

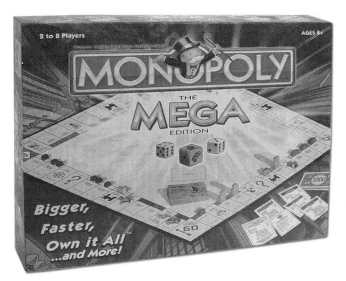

enhancements by
Winning Moves, Inc.
© 2006 Hasbro

MONOPOLY: the MEGA Edition
Includes Speed Die, Bus Tickets, Skyscrapers, Depots,
$1000 bills, 9 new Deeds, much larger Gameboard.

Mr. Monopoly pointed back to the case where I noticed the Monopoly Star Wars® Edition and dozens of other colorful games linked to cities, states, TV shows, movies and famous brands—you name it!

"If you are a native of a major U.S. city—like New York, Chicago, or Atlanta—you can buy an edition whose properties are named after places you remember in your home town. Same is true for many colleges—like Notre Dame, Ohio State, and the University of Washington. And you can always tell an official Monopoly version," he said proudly. "My picture is on it! They're made by a nice company named USAopoly."

NEW WAYS TO PLAY

"There's more," he said proudly, handing me Monopoly: The Card Game. "All the thrill of amassing properties and collecting big rents, with no wasted time." Next he showed me the game's latest DVD version. "This one includes speech and music and lets you play a virtual game against several savvy computer opponents. And if you practice the DVD game, you may well learn how to play like a champ around the real gameboard."

"What does the future hold?" I asked.

He smiled. "You can be sure that the Monopoly game will always be available in the most current electronic and video formats. Why, I wouldn't be surprised if one day it was being played in a games café on the moon!"

"The Monopoly game has come a long way," I commented. "It's one for the record books, isn't it?"

"Monopoly records? I thought you'd never ask."

Mr. Monopoly next showed me a big chart on the far wall of his den. It was titled "Monopoly Records." I had heard of many of them but still delighted in reviewing them once more. Here they are:

- Longest game ever played:
  70 days (wow!)
- Longest game in a bathtub:
  99 hours
- Longest game underwater:
  45 days!
- Longest game played upside-down:
  36 hours
- Largest outdoor game played:
  550" × 470" gameboard
  (real people served as "tokens";
  the dice were large foam cubes thrown
  from the fire escape of a building)
- Largest indoor game played:
  122" × 122" gameboard
- Smallest gameboard:
  1 inch square!

- Most expensive set ever produced in multiple copies:
  Dunhill set with solid gold playing pieces
  (value: $25,000)
- Most perishable set ever produced:
  Neiman-Marcus all-chocolate set ($600 in 1978)
- Largest price paid on eBay for most expensive Parker
  Brothers Edition:
  About $10,000 for the 1936 #25 Deluxe wood edition
- Closest call from real life:
  In 1972, Parker Brothers—and public sentiment—
  convinced Atlantic City officials not to change the
  names of Baltic and Mediterranean Avenues.
  (Both avenues have different names in some parts of
  the town. The city officials had suggested simplifying
  matters.)
- Nicest impact of progress in real life:
  The opening of Amtrak service to Atlantic City in 1989.
  (Once again, trains connected the city to the outside world.)
- Most notable achievement of the economics in the
  Monopoly game:
  No price inflation in over a half century. Values in
  the game are the same today as in 1935!

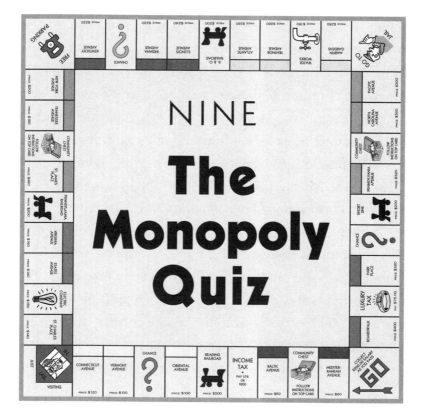

NINE

The Monopoly Quiz

"Well, it is time for your final exam," Mr. Monopoly said cheerfully. His pint-sized terrier, Scotty, was ensconced on his lap as we sat in the little man's study and sipped coffee the following morning. "I've told you all I should about the Monopoly game, save for a bit of philosophy. Now we'll see if you pass the course."

"A final exam? Mr. Monopoly, I've lived and breathed the Monopoly game these past few days. Don't you think I've learned what you've taught me? Besides, it's early in the morning . . . "

"Now, now. Maybe you have learned the basics, but your readers may have skimmed our book and missed a point or two. So here's their chance to check on their own Monopoly I.Q."

Scotty scurried away as Mr. Monopoly dipped into his ever-present briefcase and produced his neatly typed quiz. "It's actually quite straightforward. There are twenty-five multiple-choice questions. If you get twenty-three or more correct, you've earned high honors and are ready to take on a national champion. If you get eighteen to twenty-two right, you've passed and are on your way to being a good player."

"And if I get less than eighteen right, am I to repeat the course?"

"No, but you better read the pertinent parts of the book

again when you finish typing it."

"Okay, fair enough."

"Good luck, young man. Come see me again some time."

Here is Mr. Monopoly's quiz.

THE MONOPOLY FINAL EXAM

1. How many houses should there be in the game?
   a) 24
   b) 28
   c) 32
   d) 36

2. How many hotels?
   a) 10
   b) 12
   c) 14
   d) 16

3. A Community Chest card will most likely:
   a) move you to another space
   b) cost you money (a penalty)
   c) give you money (a reward)

4. A Chance card will most likely:

    a) move you to another space

    b) cost you money

    c) give you money

5. The number most frequently rolled on the dice is:

    a) 6

    b) 7

    c) 8

    d) 9

6. The two least likely numbers to roll are:

    a) 2 and 12

    b) 3 and 11

    c) 4 and 10

7. How many rolls of the dice are normally required to make a complete circuit of the board?

    a) 4

    b) 5

    c) 6

    d) 7

8. You own Illinois Avenue. An opponent owns Indiana.
You land on Kentucky. Should you buy it?
    a) yes
    b) no

9. An opponent owns States, Atlantic, and Marvin Gardens.
    Another opponent owns St. Charles and Ventnor.
    You land on Virginia. Should you buy it?
    a) definitely
    b) only if you want to
    c) no

10. An opponent owns both States and St. Charles.
    You land on Virginia. Should you buy it?
    a) definitely
    b) only if you want to
    c) no

11. You complete your first circuit around the board and
    land on Income Tax. On your circuit you earned $350
    from Chance and Community Chest cards and paid no
    penalties or rents. Should you pay 10% or $200 tax?
    a) 10%
    b) $200

12. You go to Jail at a time when eight properties remain unsold. No color-groups are completed. Should you pay $50 and get out of Jail on your very next turn, or stay in and just roll?
    a) pay $50
    b) just roll

13. You go to Jail at a time when all properties are owned and opponents own two complete color-groups. Do you pay $50 on your first turn in Jail or stay in and just roll?
    a) pay $50
    b) just roll

14. You acquire all the Light Blue properties and form the first complete color-group in the game. You have $450 in cash. What is the minimum number of houses you should build per Light Blue property?
    a) none
    b) one
    c) two
    d) three

15. You have five houses built among the Orange properties
and have just acquired the Yellow color-group. You
have $450 you wish to spend on houses. How do you
spend it?
    a) build four houses among the Orange properties
    b) build one house on each Yellow
    c) build one house on Marvin Gardens and one
       on each Orange

16. You have two houses built on each Red property.
You can afford to buy just two more houses for this
group. Where do you build them?
    a) one each on Illinois and Indiana
    b) one each on Indiana and Kentucky
    c) one each on Illinois and Kentucky

17. You have two houses built on each Orange property.
You can afford to buy just two more houses for this
group. Where do you build them?
    a) one each on New York and Tennessee
    b) one each on St. James and Tennessee
    c) one each on New York and St. James

18. You have three houses each on the Light Blues. You also have enough money to buy Hotels on each property. There are nine houses left in the Bank. One opponent owns the Yellows, the other owns the Greens. Both have decided not to buy houses at this time. What do you do?
    a) buy three additional houses
    b) buy three hotels

19. Without taking actual money needs into account, rank these properties in order of which should be mortgaged first, second, third, and fourth.
    a) Oriental (you also own Connecticut)
    b) New York (you own no other Orange property)
    c) St. Charles (you own no other Light Purple)
    d) Water Works (you do not own the Electric Company)

20. You're a bright and respected player. You have encouraged an opponent to trade with you. It is early in the game and no color-groups are yet completed. After the proposed trade, you'll end up with the Light Purples and $900 in cash; your opponent will get the Greens and have $500. Do you accept the trade?
    a) yes
    b) no

21. Same situation as in question 20, but this time it is later in the game and each player—you included—has one undeveloped color-group. After the trade, you'll have the Light Purples and $1600; your opponent will get the Greens and have $1200. Do you make the trade?
    a) yes
    b) no

22. It is the middle of the game. A proposed trade will bring you the Greens and give your opponent the Reds. You'll have $1200 to spend on houses and he'll have $1350. Neither of you has another complete color-group. Assuming you buy six houses and he buys nine, which player has the more dominant color-group as a result of the trade?
    a) you with the Greens (so the trade is a good one)
    b) he with the Reds (so the trade is questionable)

23. Which of these properties is likely to be landed on the most in a typical game?
    a) New York
    b) Illinois
    c) Boardwalk

24. Which color-group is most likely to be landed on
    in a typical game?
    a) the Railroads
    b) the Dark Blues
    c) the Reds

25. Is it better to own the Oranges and three hotels, or the
    Yellows with three houses each?
    a) the Oranges with hotels
    b) the Yellows with three houses

• • •

Fortunately, I passed the exam. To see how well you did,
see the following page for the answers. You'll also see which page
you can consult for explanation of the principle involved.

ANSWERS TO THE MONOPOLY FINAL EXAM

1. c	see p. 31
2. b	p. 31
3. c	p. 114
4. a	p. 113
5. b	p. 115
6. a	p. 115
7. c	p. 116
8. a	pp. 116–117
9. b	pp. 116–117
10. a	pp. 116–117
11. b	p. 40 *(you also earned $200 for passing GO. 10% would be $205)*
12. a	p. 118
13. b	p. 118
14. c	p. 118
15. a	p. 119
16. a	p. 120
17. c	p. 120
18. a	p. 121
19. c,d,a,b	p. 121
20. a	pp. 124–125
21. b	pp. 124–125
22. b	pp. 124–125
23. b	p. 122
24. a	p. 109
25. a	p. 109

THE TRAIN RIDE

I guess I couldn't stay away.

"All aboard!" cried the conductor. "All aboard for Atlantic City!"

The sultry afternoon weighed heavily on me as I made my way through the crowd to the waiting train. A strange mist permeated the air and I overheard a lady next to me exclaim, "Thank God for trains and Atlantic City. I can't wait to be there instead of here in this infernal city."

Where on earth was I?

I fixed my gaze upon the shiny green passenger cars of the Boardwalk Flyer and edged my way along the left side of the concrete platform towards it. The crowd swept me forward—and into—one of its waiting doors.

Breathless, I found a plush seat and sat down, loosened my tie, and got out my handkerchief to mop my brow. I looked down at my clothes. Who dressed me? I thought. Where did I get this old-fashioned suit? I looked up, and the blades of a brown fan were lazily turning above my head.

As I collected my thoughts, I also tried to remember why it was so important I catch this train. The heat bearing on my brain clouded the answer.

I couldn't help but notice a sturdy policeman handcuffed to a simian-looking character seated next to him. The policeman held a whistle between his teeth and pointed a threatening finger towards anyone who seemed ready to move past him. His nameplate read Edgar Mallory: Chief of Police, Atlantic City. "It's off to jail with him," the chief was saying to the people across the aisle. "He's Jake the Jailbird. Nasty type. Doesn't talk much either. Behind bars is where he belongs. A home for life, eh, Jake?"

Just then, three little boys ran down the aisle playing and yelling. I recognized them: the Monopoly triplets—Randy, Sandy, and my old partner Andy!

Looking around me, I saw people taking seats up and down the car, the temperature and humidity common topics of their discussion. Across the aisle to my right, one row ahead of me, sat a husky man, his balding head glistening with perspiration. A pretty red-haired woman sat next to him, staring out of the window and knitting. As a familiar-looking newsboy came by hawking papers, the man turned his profile towards me, bought a copy, and handed it to the lady at his side.

I knew his face. I was sure of it!

I had seen his picture recently.

Dumbfounded, I stood up and angled out into the aisle. The knitting lady paused, folded the inside section of the newspaper, and fanned herself with it while handing the man the front section. He began to intently study it. "Excuse me, sir," I said haltingly.

"But aren't you Charles Darrow, the man who made . . . "

I saw the headline across the top of the page. It read: Franklin Roosevelt Nominated on Fourth Ballot. Roosevelt's youthful picture appeared below the headline of the *Philadelphia Inquirer.* I saw its date: July 2, 1932!

"Yes?" the man responded. "I am Charles Darrow. Do I know you?"

I took a long look at him, then at the other passengers on this train bound with me for the World's Playground. All of us would soon be there. And so would many, many more of us— more than could fit on this train, far more than Darrow could ever dream of. All thanks to a game.

"I beg your pardon, sir," he said, snapping me out of my reverie. "I say, have we met?"

"I certainly feel we have," I said smiling.

"Then I am honored," he replied.

"I believe the honor is all mine. I want to thank you for . . ."

"Yes?"

"Well, let's just say you'll know . . . in time."

Good Luck!
Mr. Monopoly™

INDEX

Advice from champions, 172–177
Aldridge, Alvin, 169
Atlantic City
  history of, 59–60, 84–85
  jail, 88
  naming of, 60
  parking, 98
  return to, 200–202
  street map, 54
  street names, 17, 18, 20. *See also specific streets*
  street plans, 59–60
  today vs. 1935, 56–57
Atlantic, Ventnor, and Marvin Gardens, 89–94
  buying considerations, 90–92
  general information, 89–90
  group summary, 109
  Tip Sheets, 91–92
  when to build houses/hotels, 118–120
Attitude of players, 122–123
Auctions, 32–34, 47, 50, 115–116, 139

B&O Railroad. *See* Railroads
Baltic and Mediterranean, 59–69
  buying considerations, 61–69

general information, 59–60
group summary, 109
Tip Sheets, 67–68
when to build houses/hotels, 118–120
Bank
  payments to, 37
  running out of money, 61
Banker, 30–31, 32–34, 148, 149
Bankruptcy, 48–50
Barton, Robert, 22, 23–24, 134
Bayrd, Lee, 169
Bernabei, Cesare, 160–161, 163, 169, 173
Blue color-group. *See* Boardwalk and Park Place; Oriental, Vermont, and Connecticut
Boardwalk and Park Place, 103–107
  buying considerations, 105–107
  general information, 103–105
  group summary, 109
  Tip Sheets, 106–107
  when to build houses/hotels, 118–120
Building shortages
  causing, 108, 120–121
  rules, 45–47
Bunn, Jason, 166, 169, 176
Buying property
  results of failure to buy, 117

Buying property *(cont.)*
  rules, 32
  rules variation, 139
  when to buy, 116–117. *See also*
    Tip Sheets references

Champions, advice from, 172–177
Championships. *See* Tournament
    highlights; Tournaments
Chance and Community Chest
    cards, 30, 36–39, 93, 113–114,
    140
Cheng Seng Kwa, 156, 160
Color-groups
  buying considerations. *See* Tip
    Sheets, by color-group
  when and where to build
    houses/hotels, 118–120
  winning strategy, 116–117
Community Chest. *See* Chance
    and Community Chest cards
Connecticut. *See* Oriental,
    Vermont, and Connecticut
Cost considerations, 63, 109. *See
    also* Tip Sheets, by color-group
Craig, Roger, 169, 176–177

Dark Blues. *See* Boardwalk and
    Park Place
Dark Purples. *See* Baltic and
    Mediterranean

Darrow, Charles, 4
  creating famous icons, 21–22
  meeting, 201–202
  Mr. Monopoly and, 6, 7–8
  popular Monopoly story and,
    8–11, 58
  real Monopoly origin and, 18–23
Dausman, Jerry, 163, 165, 169,
    173
Dice, odds of throwing numbers,
    115
Distributing deeds/cash, for party,
    130–132
Doubles
  leaving Jail with, 41–42
  three doubles in a row, going to
    Jail with, 41, 64

Equipment
  itemized, 29–31
  knowing, for winning game,
    113–115
Evolution of Monopoly
  Charles Darrow and, 8–11, 18–23
  Elizabeth Magie-Phillips and,
    12–17, 24, 134
  Finance game and, 19–20, 24,
    144
  houses and hotels, 20
  Landlord's Game and, 14–17,
    24, 134

Parker Brothers and, 23–26
popular story about, 8–11
Robert Barton and, 23–24, 134
Single Tax idea and, 14, 17

Fernandez, Antonio, 169
Final exam (quiz), 187–197
Finance game, 19–20, 24, 144
Forbes, Jim, 166, 167, 169, 175
Fortune game, 24, 144
Free Parking, 36–37, 42, 64, 98, 139
Frequency considerations, 65–67, 109. *See also* Tip Sheets, by color-group

GET OUT OF JAIL FREE cards, 39–40, 42, 50
Glynn, Tommy, 169, 175
GO
landing on, 37, 139
passing, 38, 41
Gostomesky, Gus, 169
Green color-group. *See* Pacific, North Carolina, and Pennsylvania

History of game. *See* Evolution of Monopoly
Honor roll of champions, 169
Hoskins, Ruth, 19, 20

Hotels
evolution of, 20
knowing when/where to build, 118–120
mortgages, 48
number of, in game, 31, 46
rules, 45
selling, house shortage and, 47, 108
Houses
auctioning. See Auctions
buying and selling, 42–45. *See also* Tip Sheets, by color-group
evolution of, 20
knowing when/where to build, 118–120
mortgages, 48
number of, in game, 31, 46
rules, 42–45
shortage of, 45–47, 108, 120–121
Hyakuta, Ikuo, 169

Icons, creation of, 21–22
Immunity option, 139
Income Tax, 41–42, 117

Jacobs, Greg, 164, 165, 166, 169, 174–175
Jail
affecting frequency of landing on spaces, 64

Jail *(cont.)*
  Atlantic City jail, 88
  GET OUT OF JAIL FREE cards,
    39–40, 42, 50
  likelihood of going to, 64
  restriction options while in, 138
  rules, 41–42
  when to stay in, 118

Kentucky, Indiana, and Illinois,
  84–88
  buying considerations, 86–88
  general information, 84–85
  group summary, 109
  Tip Sheets, 86–88
  when to build houses/hotels,
    118–120
Knapp Electric, 19, 24, 134

Landlord's Game, 12–17, 24, 134
Layman, Dan, 19–20
Length of game, 37
Light Blue color-group. *See*
  Oriental, Vermont, and
  Connecticut
Light Purple color-group. *See* St.
  Charles Place, States, and
  Virginia
Local tournaments, 142–143
Luxury Tax, 13, 41, 103

Magie-Phillips, Elizabeth, 12–17,
  24, 134
Mair, John, 89, 154–156, 169
Mallet, James, 164, 166, 173
Marven Gardens, 5, 21, 90
Marvin Gardens. *See* Atlantic,
  Ventnor, and Marvin Gardens
McNally, Matthew, 169, 177
Mediterranean. *See* Baltic and
  Mediterranean
Miss America pageant, 93–94
Money
  Bank running out of, 61
  bankruptcy and, 48–50
  keeping tabs on, 115–116
  loaning, 51
  mortgages and, 48–49
  starting quantities, 30–31
  trading and, 51–52
Monopoly party, 130–140
  circulating cash and deeds, 130–132
  invitation, 138
  recipes, 137–139
  rules variations, 132, 138–140
Mortgages
  optimizing, 121–122
  rules, 48
Mr. Monopoly
  Charles Darrow and, 6, 7–8
  meeting, 2–8
  origin of, 25–26

telling history of game. *See* Evolution of Monopoly

New York. *See* St. James Place, Tennessee, and New York
North Carolina. *See* Pacific, North Carolina, and Pennsylvania
Number of players, 29–30

Object of game, 28–29, 113
Orange grouping. *See* St. James Place, Tennessee, and New York
Oren, Joost von, 169
Oriental, Vermont, and Connecticut, 69–73
  buying considerations, 69–73
  general information, 69–70
  group summary, 109
  Tip Sheets, 71–72
  when to build houses/hotels, 118–120
Osborne, R. B., 59–60

Pacific, North Carolina, and Pennsylvania, 99–103
  buying considerations, 100–103
  general information, 99–100
  group summary, 109
  Tip Sheets, 101–103
  when to build houses/hotels, 118–120

Parker Brothers
  popular Monopoly story and, 8–10
  real Monopoly origin and, 22–26
  tournament points, 147
Parker, George, 14–15, 23, 24
Park Place. *See* Boardwalk and Park Place
Party. *See* Monopoly party
Patent
  of Landlord's Game, 12–13, 15, 24
  of Monopoly, 23–24
Payback considerations, 62, 63, 65–66, 109. *See also* Tip Sheets, by color-group
Payoff %, 65–66, 109. *See also* Tip Sheets, by color-group
Pennsylvania. *See* Pacific, North Carolina, and Pennsylvania
Pennsylvania Railroad. *See* Railroads
Peters, Gary, 168, 169, 176
Pitney, Jonathan, 59–60
Player conduct, 122–123
Power considerations, 65–66. *See also* Tip Sheets, by color-group
Probability, of landing on spaces. *See* Frequency considerations; Tip Sheets, by color-group

Purple color-group. *See* Baltic and Mediterranean; St. Charles Place, States, and Virginia

Quick auctions, 139
Quiz, 187–197

Railroads, 94–99
  advance token to nearest one, 38
  buying considerations, 96–98
  general information, 55–56, 94, 95
  group summary, 109
  Tip Sheets, 97–98
Reading Railroad. *See* Railroads
Recipes for Monopoly party, 133–137
Records, 185–186
Red color-group. *See* Kentucky, Indiana, and Illinois
Rent, 34–35, 38. *See also* specific properties; Tip Sheets, by color-group
  estimating payments, 116
  immunity option, 139
Repole, Angelo, 157–159, 166, 172
Rules. *See also* Hotels; Houses
  auctions, 32–34
  bankruptcy, 48–50
  building shortages, 44–47, 108
  buying property, 32

Chance and Community Chest cards, 30, 36–40
  equipment, 29–31
  Free Parking, 36–37, 42
  houses, 43–45
  Income Tax, 41–42
  jail, 40–41, 42–43
  length of game, 37
  mortgages, 48
  number of players, 29–30
  object of game, 28–29
  paying rent, 34–35
  starting play, 31–32
  starting quantities of money, 30–31
  time limit/short games, 143
  trading, 51–52
  variations, 132, 138–140

Score sheets
  home game score sheet, 204
  sample tournament score sheet, 145
Short games, 140
Short Line. *See* Railroads
Starting play, 31–32
State champions, 142–143
States. *See* St. Charles Place, States, and Virginia
St. Charles Place, States, and Virginia, 73–76

buying considerations, 80–83
general information, 73–74
Tip Sheets, 75–76
when to build houses/hotels,
    118–120
St. James Place, Tennessee, and
    New York, 80–83
buying considerations, 80–83
general information, 80
group summary, 109
Tip Sheets, 81–83
when to build houses/hotels,
    118–120
Strategies. *See* Winning strategies
Streets. *See* Atlantic City; specific
    street names

Tennessee. *See* St. James Place,
Tennessee, and New York
Terman, Dana, 157, 159–161, 162,
    163, 169, 172
Time limit games, 140
Tip Sheets, by color-group
Dark Blues (Boardwalk, Park
    Place), 106–107
Dark Purples (Baltic,
    Mediterranean), 63
Greens, 101–103
Light Blues (Oriental, Vermont,
    Connecticut), 71–72
Light Purples (St. Charles,

States, Virginia), 75–76
Oranges (St. James Place,
    Tennessee, New York), 81–83
Railroads, 97–98
Reds (Kentucky, Indiana,
    Illinois), 86–88
summary by property group, 109
Yellows (Atlantic, Ventnor,
    Marvin Gardens), 91–92
Tip Sheets, considerations
cost considerations, 63
frequency considerations, 63
payback considerations, 62, 63,
    65–66
power considerations, 65–66
Todd, Charles, 20–21
Tokens, 29
Tournament highlights, 153–168
    1975, 153–155
    1977, 155–156
    1980, 157–162
    1983, 163–165
    1985, 165–166
    1987, 167–168
Tournaments, 142–169
determining assets in, 144
honor roll of champions, 169
local, 142–143
points to remember, 147
score sheet sample, 145
state champions, 143–144

Tournaments, *(cont.)*
.U.S. championship, 146, 148
World Tournament, 148–152
Trading
effective trades, 124–126
immunity option, 139
rules, 50–51
Turns to go around board, 116

U. S. championship, 146,
148
Utilities, 77–79
buying considerations, 77–79
general information, 77
group summary, 109
rent amounts, 38
Tip Sheets, 78–79

Ventnor. *See* Atlantic, Ventnor,
and Marvin Gardens
Vermont. *See* Oriental, Vermont,
and Connecticut
Versions of game, 181–186
Virginia. *See* St. Charles Place,
States, and Virginia

Winning strategies, 113–127
advice from champions, 172–177
causing building shortages, 108,
120–121
estimating rent payments, 116
knowing color group pros/cons,
117
knowing dice odds, 115
knowing equipment well,
113–115
monitoring money, 115–116
optimizing mortgages, 121–122
player conduct, 122–123
remembering object of game,
113
trading effectively, 124–126
when and where to build
houses/hotels, 118–120
when to buy, 116–117
when to pay income tax, 117
when to stay in jail, 118
Woo, Christopher, 179
World Tournament, 150–154

Yellow grouping. *See* Atlantic,
Ventnor, and Marvin Gardens

ABOUT THE AUTHORS

Mr. Monopoly is the leading expert on the world's most popular board game—the Monopoly game—and has been since 1936! Often called "the Monopoly Man" or "the Chairman of the Board," the venerable financier has here consented to share his secrets for the very first time. Born in Atlantic City (in a year he chooses not to specify), he still lives nearby with his wife Madge, who frequently babysits nephews Andy, Randy, and Sandy.

Philip Orbanes has made the games business his career, spurred by his very first encounter with the Monopoly game at age eight. A graduate of Case Institute of Technology, he headed the research and development department at Parker Brothers for many years and is currently president of specialty game maker Winning Moves, Inc. He has authored three other books on games and has served as Chief Judge at national and world Monopoly tournaments since 1979. He and his wife Anna have two grown sons, both of whom are avid gamers.